Global Sustainable Capitalism

Global Sustainable Capitalism

Mario Svigir, Harry Xia, and
Marcus Goncalves

 BUSINESS EXPERT PRESS

Global Sustainable Capitalism

First published in 2020 by
Business Expert Press, LLC
222 East 46th Street, New York, NY 10017
www.businessexpertpress.com

ISBN-13: 978-1-94744-159-0 (paperback)
ISBN-13: 978-1-94744-160-6 (e-book)

Business Expert Press Economics and Public Policy Collection

Collection ISSN: 2463-761X (print)
Collection ISSN: 2163-7628 (electronic)

Cover and interior design by Exeter Premedia Services Private Ltd., Chennai, India

First edition: 2020

10 9 8 7 6 5 4 3 2 1

Printed in the United States of America.

Dedication

To all International Business students at Nichols College, for the lengthy discussions about global trade, foreign affairs, and international business as a whole during the semester, including forms of sustainable capitalism. To my beloved wife Carla, always patient and caring with me during these time-consuming projects. To my son Samir, who brings me so much pride; and to my other two children, Andrea and Joshua (in memory), also treasures in my life, for which I count the days to join. To God, be the glory!

Marcus Goncalves

Summer 2019

This book is dedicated to my wife Vivian and my son Vinson, for their kindness and endless support. Thanks for always being there for me.

Harry Xia

Summer 2019

To all those who work toward and live in accordance of awareness that we all are ultimately human brothers and sisters, having only one joint home, Environment, and that this ultimately means that we also share the human history and are bound to share hopefully more sustainable future. To all of my colleagues and students at the University. Last but not least to my family and God who keeps inspiring and aspiring me to boldly go where there are no traditional paths of progress in thought, and for action. I thank Marcus Goncalves for teaming up with me and Danielle Doty for all the research assistance she has provided on this project.

Mario Svigir

Summer 2019

Abstract

Sustainable capitalism knowledge is often assumed for exclusive association with information about some forms of environmental crises. When we speak of sustainable and unsustainable, we speak of a systemic crisis of long-term dimension in the economy and business models, on all levels. We talk of local to a global crisis, with detrimental effects on humans and the environment, as well as economic organizations, of various kinds, often forfeiting any economic, social, and environmental future. The long-term crisis is not just a crisis of long-term investment, but also a crisis of human and ecological capital.

The authors propose a new conceptual business model, polycentric, at many levels. This research is an attempt to contribute to the global alliance for such sustainable capitalism in the making. In part, this is an ambitious undertaking, as the authors analyzed vital UN documents on sustainable development, as part of what they advocate as sustainable capitalism, as a systemic response to existing shortcomings of the present model. This text attempts to educate global stakeholders about the importance, the rationale, and the pathway to introduce sustainable capitalism into global economics and business models.

Keywords

capitalism; sustainable capitalism; crony capitalism; capitalism 2.0; reform of capitalism; market competition against abuse of markets

Contents

Preface

Sustainable capitalism knowledge is often assumed for exclusive association with information about some forms of environmental crises. When we speak of sustainable and unsustainable, we speak of a systemic crisis of long-term dimension in the economy and business models, on all levels. We talk of local to global crisis, with detrimental effects on humans and the environment, as well as economic organizations, of various kinds, often forfeiting any economic, social, and environmental future. The long-term crisis is a crisis not only of long-term investment, but also of human and ecological capital.

The unsustainability of the present social and global environmental crises is placing the financial state of the world in jeopardy. Melting of polar ice caps is coinciding today with a worldwide rush toward protectionisms of various sorts. Global geostrategic tensions are coinciding with income inequalities and acidification of oceans. Desertification is spreading along with global terrorism threats. Issues related to global economics and social and environmental sustainability have become the biggest question for global business survival, as these nonconnected events are, in fact, very much connected. Issues such as environmental fairness or social justice resurface as elements of more sustainable capitalism and its subsequent business model. Again, global interconnectivity calls us toward discernment of new forms of collective responsibilities and toward sharing in the global chains in the sustainable manner and format of businesses.

In that sense, sustainable capitalism is not about the abolition of markets or financial gains, state of the technology, or modern digitalization of the world. The authors of this book argue that it is about finding new paths, more whole and broader routes for creating wealth and income while preserving and nurturing human beings and natural habitats.

The authors propose a new conceptual business model, polycentric at many levels. This research is an attempt to contribute to the global alliance for such sustainable capitalism in the making. In part, this is an ambitious undertaking, as the authors analyzed vital UN documents on sustainable development, as part of what they advocate as sustainable capitalism, as a systemic response to existing shortcomings of the present model. This text attempts to educate global stakeholders about the importance, rationale, and pathway to introduce sustainable capitalism into global economics and business models.

This book proposes a comprehensive theoretical subject analysis. It also advocates the potential for the introduction of sustainable capitalism into practices of various kinds. It examines the history and potential development of a new global sustainable business model while proposing a policy dialogue about it. Overall, this book attempts to better understand current, and future, prospects of sustainable capitalism in the making and its business models as a response to many of the present global geopolitical, economic, and environmental challenges.

Acknowledgments

Many people helped us during the process of researching and writing this book. It would be difficult to keep track of them all. Therefore, to all that we have forgotten to list, please don't hold it against us!

We thank Dr. Patrick Barron, professor at the Graduate School of Banking at the University of Wisconsin, Madison, and of Austrian economics at the University of Iowa, in Iowa City, for the insights his work provides on the issue. We would also like to thank Mr. Bo-Young Lin, from the Graduate Institute of International and Development Studies and the United Nations Conference on Trade and Development (UNCTAD) for his support and insights.

CHAPTER 1

The Limits of Current Global Capitalism: An Introduction

Overview

Not only in the authors' teaching experience, in various disciplines, but also in Dr. Svigir's economics consulting engagements with policy makers at the European Commission (EC), we typically assumed that the quality of knowledge and debates regarding macroeconomics is continuously neglected at large or omitted altogether. It is either reserved for academic discussions or misplaced in the course of the overall understanding of a variety of emergent phenomena in business and economics regarding globalization. That is a shame since macroeconomics, as a discipline, is very much about the part of economics concerned with the large-scale or general economic factors, such as interest rates and national productivity. Macroeconomics is at the heart of the debate on sustainable global capitalism, as it encompasses the whole economic system of a country (and the world!), especially with regard to general levels of output and income and the interrelations among sectors of the economy. In any part of the world, businesses cannot become genuinely sustainable unless the economic system within which they operate is itself supportable of the behaviors that enable viable business practice.

The limitations inherent within the current framework for capitalism need to be investigated. There is a need to explore what might be required to promote a genuinely balanced global economy, global sustainable capitalism, its risks and opportunities for business, and how business leaders may contribute to it. There is also a need to understand better the limitations of the old economic ways and the call for a new operating capitalist system.

Capitalism 1.0

After the collapse of communism and the breakdown of the old Soviet Union, over 20 years ago, global capitalism seems to have triumphed. Capitalism, post-Soviet Union, which we dubbed here "Capitalism 1.0," became a sort of a legal system that safeguards private property and permits free trade in competitive markets across the globe. At least theoretically, this form of capitalism was supposed to enable individuals to pursue their self-interest freely. Assuming competition restrains these self-interests, society would always benefit from lower prices and broader choices. The problem, however, as illustrated in the cartoon of Figure 1.1, is that dominant forces of self-interest have a natural tendency to collusion and corruption. In other words, with a few exceptions, capitalists, large multinational corporations, and interest groups tend to seek power and use it to rig the market in their favor to the detriment of society.

Figure 1.1 Crony capitalism leads to corruption and collusion

Source: http://hermes-press.com

In the 1987 film, "Wall Street," Michael Douglas' character Gordon Gekko notoriously said that, in capitalism, "it is a zero-sum game: Somebody wins, somebody loses. Money itself isn't lost or made; it's simply transferred from one perception to another." Messages such as these, degrading free markets, have always been widespread, but have gotten ever more pervasive with films like Michael Moore's "Capitalism: A Love Story" to the more recent documentary "Inside Job," all shaming the true merits of a free, capitalist society.

Adam Smith, the intellectual father of capitalism, observed over more than 200 years ago that the competitive market, as if by an "invisible hand," transforms self-interest into a force for the public good. He explained how competition maximizes productivity and social welfare by assuring the optimal allocation of capital and labor in the overall economy. But, as Michael Moore puts it, "This economic system they call capitalism has no moral or ethical core to it," nor, he says, is it democratic. Proponents of such absurd ideas are often the first to provide solutions, and what better a solution than the benevolence of big government to fight the evils of Big Oil and Walmart? Not quite, though. Frederic Bastiat's work "That Which Is Seen, and That Which Is Not Seen" shows just how easy it is to ignore the unforeseen consequences of any action, including big government. Contrary to their own beliefs, opponents of the free market are mistaken when saying that big government is the solution to "evil" businesses. In fact, the very opposite is true—government officials and business leaders have increasingly gotten cozy with another and not for the better. When corporations get handouts at the expense of taxpayers, there is a problem, and that problem has nothing to do with capitalism. That problem lies in what economist Russ Roberts and many others call crony capitalism or corporatism.

Karl Marx argued that capitalism would eventually collapse because of this and other internal contradictions of the system. Marx believed that the distribution of income and wealth would become increasingly unequal under capitalism. When the workers could no longer tolerate being exploited by the capitalists, a communist revolution would result. Initially, Marx said, there would be a political transition period in which the state would not be anything more than a revolutionary dictatorship of the proletariat, which would seize all private property from the capitalists on behalf of the working class. Eventually, all class distinctions would disappear, causing the state to wither away and being replaced by an international, and apparently democratic, commune of the proletariat.

Crony capitalism has been a pervasive feature not only in the American political economy but also all over the world. History is besieged with examples of industries turning to government to get the upper hand, from window manufacturers and "green" energy businesses to labor unions and banks. Friedrich Hayek's seminal work in the problem of knowledge has shown that no central planner has the wisdom to pick which is right and which is wrong. The question of knowledge is best left for the free market, and for prices to honestly reflect real values.

Marx also argued that a communist society would deliver the highest welfare for most people, at least in theory. In practice, the results have been devastating. There is a movement among young people across the globe glamorizing communism, one of the harshest societies anyone could live in. In the United Kingdom, an increasingly popular phrase "I'm literally a communist," argued by 26-year-old activist and lecturer Ash Sarkar to Piers Morgan on Good Morning Britain, tells the story of British individuals in a capitalist society who are seeing their peers trapped in jobs which don't pay enough to survive, with spiraling debt and few opportunities.

Social equality and egalitarianism are attractive words fused in a nightmare. It is not possible to have equality when a single political party conditions you to praise and support it to get what you want. No doubt, Capitalism 1.0 has genuine and harmful flaws, but just as a single among many examples, if we were to reflect on Romania of the 1980s, we will realize what was beyond the egalitarianism motto. Romania has suffered from a rough communism period which ruled for more than 40 years. Under the Romanian People's Republic, the state followed Eastern Bloc ideology with only one leading political party and nationalization of all banks and large organizations. The Constitution was nothing but a form of deceit. It provided a series of hypothetical freedoms like religion, press, political options, meetings, and protests that were not maintained in practice. Citizens were forced to settle with what the government dictated or face dangerous, often deadly, consequences. The leader of the Romanian Communist Party, Nicolae Ceausescu, went out into history as one of the most extreme communist dictators of all time. In 1982, Ceausescu had only one goal, to pay the external debt Romania had previously acquired.

The most abusive era started with him imposing the austerity policy that led to economic stagnation. This encompassed extreme food rations, massive queues in front of a grocery store hours before its opening, and a considerable reduction of electricity and heating in people's houses.

What is most interesting is that a survey conducted in 2014 showed that 61 percent of Romanians believe that people had a better life during the communism era than in the present. Similarly, 68 percent of people born after 1989, so after the end of communism, share the same view. The flaws of modern capitalist society under Capitalism 1.0, such as corruption or poverty, have led to fond memories of the times when people were not allowed to be against the party, to express their own views, to travel whenever and wherever they wanted to, or to have bread and meat in their house every single day. These are things that we tend to take for granted and cannot imagine how such a limited and harshly enforced system could rule lives.

Another example is the destructive consequences of Soviet communism, becoming more evident as time progresses. The ecological destruction has been immense. Corruption and incompetence have stifled economic creativity. Central planning has produced massive economic stagnation and waste. Technology is often primitive and even hazardous, as demonstrated by the Chernobyl disaster. Products are substandard in quality and scarce in supply. The standard of living is subpar, and health conditions are among the lowest in the world.

While both Adam Smith and Karl Marx agreed on a few fundamental concepts, they diverged on the method of production of goods and services and distribution of resources. Whereas Karl Marx went so far as suggesting revolution by the proletariat against the bourgeoisie for a more just, equitable society, Adam Smith preferred stability and peace over revolution. While Adam Smith's envisioned ideal society would not distribute resources equitably or eliminate gaping wealth levels between the different classes in a society, Marx's ideal economy would produce, according to the directives from a central authority, and distribute resources according to the needs of the public. In his idyllic economy, Marx envisioned the elimination of class distinctions and appropriate valuation of a worker's effort, which is not possible in a capitalistic society in the presence of profit-seeking capitalists who deprive workers of their full share of earnings, according to Marx.

By global income percentile, 2011 prices at PPP*

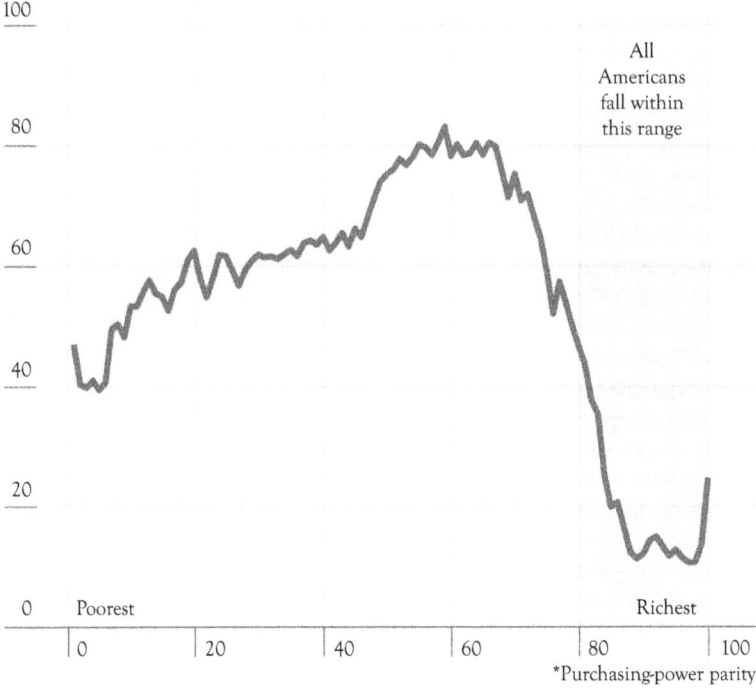

Figure 1.2 Global income percentile 1993–2016

Source: The Economist, https://economist.com/open-future/2018/04/16/
fixing-the-flaws-in-todays-capitalism

Smith's prognostications, however, have been abnormally accurate. It is in this predictive sense that recent events mark the triumph of Adam Smith's ideas over those of Karl Marx. Capitalism, in principle, has outlasted communism. Although Capitalism 1.0 tends toward the inadequate distribution of income and wealth, it has delivered far larger prosperity to far more people than any other economic system. Moreover, in an ironic twist, it indeed confounded communists—most notably Marx, Engels, and Lenin—who predicted that capitalism would eventually collapse. Smith did warn that special interests could do a great deal of harm, but he believed that the power of capitalism would prevail.

Smith acknowledged that in a capitalist economy, nowadays a global capitalism one, some individuals would likely become much wealthier than others. He argued that as long as there was economic development, the rich would get richer, but the poor would also be better off. Marx, of course, predicted that the poor would become more miserable. Interestingly enough, the number of wealthy individuals in communist China, the world's largest economy in purchase parity power (PPP), or second biggest in dollar terms, has grown exponentially over the past decade. This is possible thanks to a sort of *Sino-capitalist system*, where the Chinese government is allowing an economic and political system in which the country's trade and industry are being controlled, at least in part (not to be confused with a free market), by private owners for profit, rather than by the state. China has embarked on a privatization process of its state-owned enterprises (SOE), allowing for at least a freer market.

Nonetheless, despite the advantages of the capitalism principle, as portrayed by Smith, Capitalism 1.0 needs to be reformulated. Wealthy nations across the globe show evidence that the economy no longer works

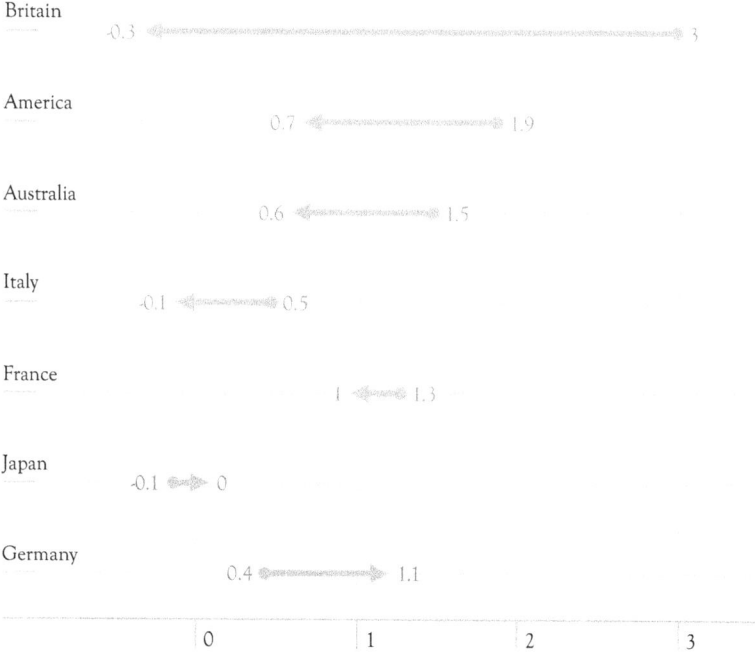

Figure 1.3 Real-wage growth, average annual % change, 1998–2008, 2008–2016

Source: The Economist, https://economist.com/open-future/2018/04/16/fixing-the-flaws-in-todays-capitalism

for many of its people. Globalization has brought enormous benefits to the world as a whole, but middle-income people in rich countries seem to have fared poorly in recent years, as shown in Figure 1.2.

As depicted in Figure 1.3, high unemployment is also a major problem, afflicting much of Europe and most of the world's economies. The United States and the United Kingdom have (relatively) low unemployment but have seen a big rise in insecure work. Real-wage growth across the rich world has been measly.

Negative Impacts of Individual Interests

The savings and loan crisis in the United States is an extraordinarily good example of the damage that individual interests can do. The fact that the U.S. economy has continued to grow despite this and many other shocks, including the 1987 stock market crash, the 1989 collapse of the

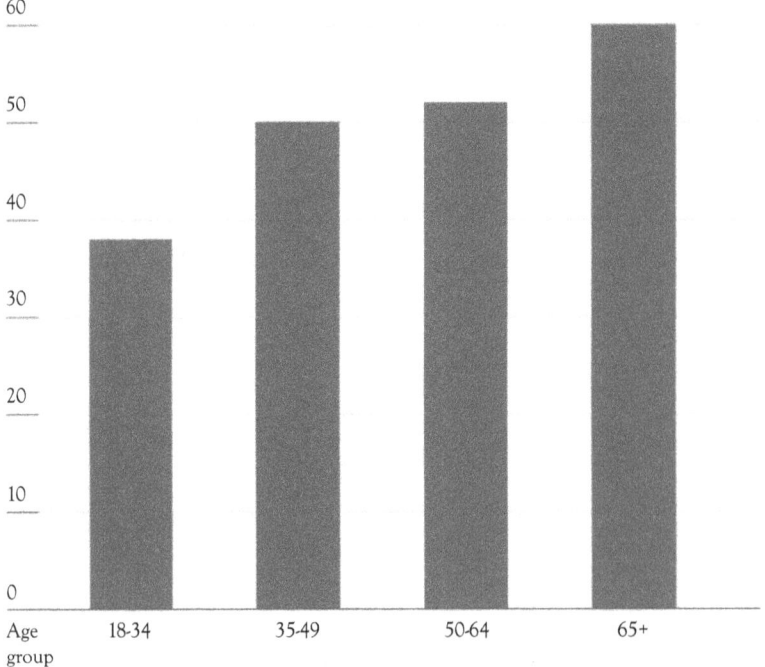

Figure 1.4 Support for capitalism in America, 2016, %

Source: The Economist, https://economist.com/open-future/2018/04/16/
fixing-the-flaws-in-todays-capitalism

junk-bond market, and the massive collapse of the global financial markets in 2007 to 2011, strongly supports Smith's unswerving faith in the resilience of the capitalist system.

Not surprisingly, however, many hard-working people feel alienated. The feeling that the economy does not work for ordinary people has driven many toward populist causes, including Brexit and Boris Johnson, Donald Trump, and the National Front in France. Support for capitalism among young people is low, as shown in Figure 1.4.

Noteworthy is the fact that competition for wealth and social status was hardly created by the capitalist system. People have always competed for these things. Thanks to capitalism, though, this competition is now less violent, and true poverty is easier to avoid.

Hoodwinking the Economy

Nowadays, Smith is often remembered as a champion of the capitalist society, but nothing could be further from the truth. Contrary to the conventional view, he did not advocate unrestrained capitalism, and he indeed was not an admirer of capitalists. Smith repeatedly warned that in pursuing their self-interests, capitalists tend to join in powerful special interest groups. These coalitions seek political influence to promote public policies that benefit themselves, often at the expense of public interest. In his writings, Smith often railed against the capitalists and accused them of hoodwinking the nation. He frequently observed that the benefits of merchants and manufacturers always run contrary to those of the general public. Because their interests are at odds with the public interest, capitalists advocate policies that they claim to be good for the entire nation, but in fact, are suitable only for themselves.

These are hardly the words of a champion of the unrestrained pursuit of self-interest. To counter the political manipulations of the special interests, Smith believed that selfishness could be disciplined and channeled in socially beneficial directions. He saw three mechanisms that together would do the job: self-discipline, the competitive market, and a system of justice. Individuals have the aptitude to be both good and bad, Smith argued, suggesting that we either tend to agree or disagree with our behavior, depending on the circumstances, on how it benefits us or not. Smith recognized that self-discipline was not enough and that many people would violate their moral conscience and act in ways harmful to society if there were not at least two other checks—the competitive market and a system of justice.

Today, in the United States and throughout the world, the clearest example of the excesses of Capitalism 1.0 and the destructive influence of special interests is the global financial crisis, which by 2013 had already cost more than $22 trillion. It was by far the biggest and most spectacular failure in the entire financial history of the United States, with dire consequences for the whole global economy, especially for advanced economies, and by (extended) contagion, emerging markets, although not as much to frontier economies.

Savings and investments in the American money market by emerging economies, especially the BRICS (Brazil, Russia, India, China, and South Africa) but China as it refused Washington's recommendations to open up its markets without restrains, financed the excessive consumption of the United States in the early 2000s, which indirectly led to a global financial crisis. The crisis started from the real estate mortgage market, with disrupting processes beginning in the American financial market, which contradicted all previously known equilibrium theories of every school of economics. The field of economics has yet to come up with models or empirical approaches to explain this (new) disequilibrium. Naturally, the issues of reasonable risks and greed, credit ratings and shareholder control, limited liability, and market regulations are aspects which cannot be ignored.

The global financial crisis, estimated to have led to trillions of dollars of loss all over the world, was not caused by a war or a significant recession. It was caused by the shadow banking system of the United States, including but not limited to greed and predatory practices of the investment banks, hedge funds, and supermarket-owned banks, as well as the elegant mathematical models that are based on irrelevant premises and were not even truthfully understood by most financial managers. At the time, an explanation was given, very casually and with not much transparency, by suggesting that the crisis was caused by the liquidity shortage of the American banks, which was the result of the overvaluation of assets. In other words, the most critical causing factor was never mentioned, which was the focal point of the anatomy of the crisis, namely, the greedy and irresponsible Wall Street investment companies.

These financial institutions transformed barely documented sub-prime mortgage loans, designed for clients with weak credit rating into exotic and poisonous financial products through multiple leverages. Several financial institutions were involved, which included, apart from American banks and hedge funds, other institutions such as Lehman Brothers, Goldman Sachs, Salomon Brothers, J.P. Morgan, Citibank, Wells Fargo, AIG, and Bear Stearns. In addition, several foreign banks operating on Wall Street, including the Swiss UBS, the German Deutsche Bank, the English Barclay's, were all involved in these deals. Their global branch networks were equally situated in advanced economies such as Japan, the United Kingdom, and Germany, as well as in the emerging ones such as China, Brazil, and South Korea, to name a few. These financial institutions sold utterly unfounded expectations and unsecured stocks to noncreditworthy middle-class investors for large sums and earned astronomic amounts with proprietary trading. The leverage trade in the derivatives of the real estate mortgages was extensive even when the fallacious rating of these derivatives by the American Moody's, S&P, Fitch, and so on became visible and it was increasingly likely that the American real estate market bubble was going to burst.

Gauging the damage from the global financial crisis is, therefore, not candid, even with the benefit of reflection provided by 10 years of history, because the counter-factual of what might have happened in its absence is inscrutable. However, as argued in December 2018 by David Turner and Patrice Ollivaud, at the Organization for Economic Cooperation and Development (OECD) Economics Department, a naïve, but commonly adopted approach of comparing the postcrisis path of GDP with the precrisis trend exaggerates the cost and can lead to misleading policy conclusions. Such an approach is akin to treating the crisis as a meteorite from outer space, which is entirely unrelated or exogenous to preceding macroeconomic developments. This is improbable because the precrisis trend in GDP involved unsustainable trends in asset prices, most obviously house prices, driven by an extended period of rapid excessive credit growth across most of the advanced economies.

According to the latest analyses (see Cassidy 2010), the global financial crisis was directly caused by the inefficient market allocation of international, primarily Chinese, savings flowing into the United States. The vast liquidity abundance amassed in the American financial sector was used to enhance American living standards and finance the disproportionately high consumption of the American economy, instead of productive goals or the efficient transformation of the struggling American industry's production structure, such as by making the American steel production or motor industry more competitive. The bursting of the IT bubble in the second half of the 1990s, followed by significant cuts in IT investments, was an additional factor in this tendency. This process and many of its interim developments finally led to the credit crisis on the real estate mortgage market as well as the credit card market. First, a minor economic recession occurred in the American economy, and then the world was pushed into a financial crisis by the high appetite for risk demonstrated by investors from all over the world. To date, very little is known about the International Monetary Fund's (IMF) role or activities during the crisis. The IMF undertook an exponentially more significant task in the management of the crisis (see Csáki 2009) and presumably absorbed even higher proceeds than during the Bretton Woods era. Consequently, if we may say so, the IMF is one of the winners of the crisis.

The Global Financial Crisis

The crisis and its management were analyzed by numerous scholars, investigative journalists, economists, book authors, and the media, both in the United States and abroad. These analyses are mostly dominated by macroeconomic papers and discussions, focusing primarily on the role of the contradictory Keynes and neoclassic schools and the crisis of economic science (Móczár 2010a). Mellár (2010) undertook an even more significant assignment when he briefly described all textbook macro models and reached a conclusion that, as these models did not include the financial sector, they could not predict the financial crisis.

In our view, the central lasting macroeconomic damage from the global financial crisis is accounted for by lost productivity. The OECD suggests that for most member countries experiencing a banking crisis, most of this lost productivity was considered for by lower growth in capital per worker, rather than lower total factor productivity (TFP), as depicted in Figure 1.5. The loss in capital per worker illustrates how a severe adverse demand shock can be transformed into an adverse supply shock via an accelerator effect on investment that then reduces the capital stock. Also, increasing evidence, including from corporate-level research, suggests that many nations where interest rates were particularly low in the precrisis period, especially in Southern Europe, experienced a substantial misallocation of capital. These countries are also among those that experienced a more abrupt postcrisis adjustment in capital stock growth. The fall in capital stock growth was also exacerbated in some countries by cutbacks in public investment after the crisis.

There is a broad consensus that this crisis could not have developed without any prior events. However, opinions differ as to how long we should go back in history. Michael Lewis, an American bestseller author, who writes for the general public about scandalous American finances,

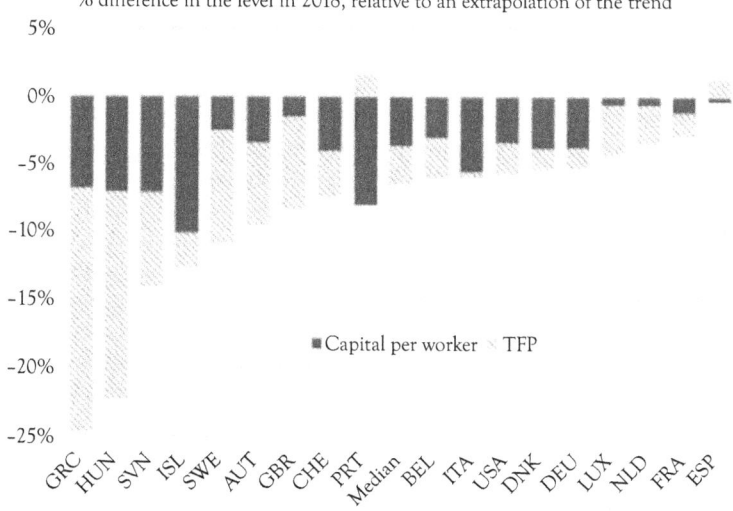

Figure 1.5 Estimates of the loss in trend productivity due to the global financial crisis

Source: Ollivaud, P., Y. Guillemette and D. Turner (2018).
Notes: The Countries shown are those OECD countries experiencing a banking crisis after the GFC. The bars show the estimated deflection in components of trend productivity relative to pre-crisis trend distinguishing between a capital per worker and a TFP component

would go back to his book *Liar's Pocker* (1982). Notwithstanding, he culminates the predatory practices of Wall Street in another of his book titled *The Big Short* (2010), revealing the Wall Street bombastic deal of securitization of mortgages, invented by the Salomon Brothers, which took off and saturated the markets by the mid-1990s. On the other hand, one of the few economists who warned about the impending crisis, Rajan (2005) from Chicago, would go back only to the crisis waves sweeping across the emerging markets of the 1990s. These waves caused the collapse of the economies of East Asia, made the stock exchange and real estate market twin bubble burst in Japan, rendered Russia insolvent, and created considerable financial difficulties for Argentina, Brazil, and Turkey. The emerging countries opted for the simplest possible solution to avoid the crash: they became a lot more cautious in external borrowing, their governments and companies cut back on capital investments, and their households spent less. With such restrictions, these emerging countries soon turned from net importers into net exporters of financial investments.

With the collapse of communism and the disintegration of the old Soviet Union, global capitalism had apparently succeeded. Economists point to declining growth rates, technological lag, and general inefficiency of the communist economic system as the decisive factors in bringing the regime down. An alternative argument, however, is that it was not so much a financial crisis that forced reform, as the drive for improvement in itself created a political crisis. Whatever the reasons, the clash of ideologies appeared to be over.

While the western capitalism is the only example of capitalism as the world understands it, good or bad, aside from communism, the only means of meeting people's collective needs, for allocating scarce resources and distributing wealth, it has also been an example of the excesses. Capitalism has also been blamed for its contribution to the global financial meltdown, which has led the world, especially the United States, into the most prolonged and most profound global financial crisis in living memory. Since then, western capitalism is still groaning at the seams, suffering a crisis of liquidity, reliability, and confidence, and is naturally undergoing a wise degree of introspection.

So, what is wrong with Capitalism 1.0? After all, historically, it has delivered unprecedented growth and prosperity, hasn't it? The challenges facing the planet today are unique and extraordinary: climate change, water scarcity, poverty, disease, growing inequality of income and wealth, demographic shifts, transborder and internal migration, urbanization, and a global economy in a state of constant dramatic volatility and flux, to name but a few. While governments and civil society will need to be part of the solution to these massive challenges, ultimately, it will be corporations and investors that will mobilize the capital needed to overcome them.

Umair Haque, economist, author, and blogger, points out in his excellent book *The New Capitalist Manifesto* that real growth in the developed economies reached a contrary inflection point decades ago and has been steadily slowing for half a century. David Korten, U.S. economist, author, and former Harvard professor, also shows us that any perceived growth has also been more of an illusion. He dubbed it "unsustainable phantom wealth," based on financial bubbles, abuse of power by banks to create credit from nothing, corporate asset stripping, baseless credit ratings, and creative accounting. The world of financial stability, environmental sustainability, economic justice, and peace that most psychologically healthy people want is possible if we replace a defective operating system that values only money, seeks to monetize every relationship, and pits each person in competition with every other for dominance.

A better plan, as many economists have been arguing, is to force bankrupt banks into government receivership. As part of the sale and distribution of assets to meet creditor claims, these banks should be broken up and their local branches sold to local investors. These new, individual community banks and mutual savings and loan associations should be chartered to serve the needs of the masses, also known as Main Street, through lending to local manufacturers, merchants, farmers, and homeowners within a stable regulatory framework.

Under Capitalism 1.0, even with its *economic growth,* more limited in size than perhaps realized, one still needs to account for the trickle-down effect, with prosperity reaching only a privileged few, and a decline in real income for the majority. In fact, from 1980 to 2005, the highest-earning one percent of the U.S. population increased its share of taxable income from 9 to 19 percent, with most of the gain going to the top one-tenth of that one percent. This situation is not unique to the United States, as the case in the United Kingdom is worse still, with the fastest-growing gap between rich and poor in the developed world. The system is designed to concentrate wealth.

Whichever way one looks, Capitalism 1.0 has failed to create shared prosperity, not to mention the fact we have not even considered the environment yet, although we must. Some of the most widely recognized causes of the crash in capital markets are also the principal, underlying causes of the environmental crisis we now face. We seem not to realize how far beyond our means we have been living, environmentally as well as financially. And we still do not correctly understand the way those two spheres of human activity are connected. The shock to the system, causing the near collapse of our global banking industry, has been traumatic. Even so, that is nothing compared to the near-imminent collapse of the ecological systems on which we depend on, particularly a stable climate.

In 2018, according to Oxfam, 2,200 billionaires worldwide saw their wealth grow by 12 percent, while the poorest half of the world saw its wealth fall by 11 percent, which is hard to believe at a time when global poverty is consistently falling. Figure 1.6 provides a region composed of the global wealth distribution in 2018.

The rich are definitely getting way richer, which is a problem, but it is also true that the world's poorest people are getting less poor, which

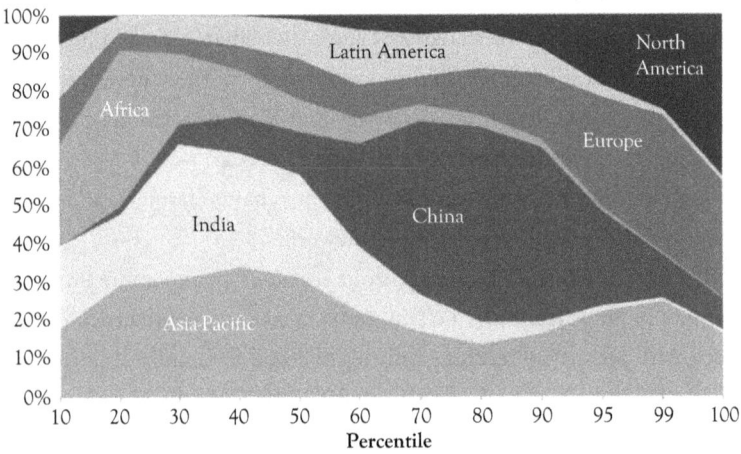

Figure 1.6 Region composition of the global wealth distribution in 2018

Source: Credit Suisse Global Wealth Report 2018

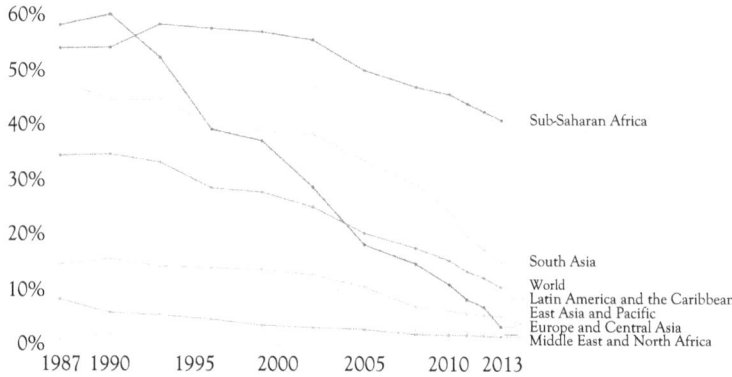

Figure 1.7 Share of the global population living in extreme poverty, by world region

Source: World Bank, 2016

can be verified in a variety of statistics, at least the World Bank's estimates of how many people live on less than $1.90 a day (based on 2011 PPP prices), as shown in Figure 1.7. This data is based on household surveys, which take years to collect, so it is out of date at any given time, but economic growth in India, China, and even sub-Saharan Africa suggests that the progress continued through to the present day.

It is astonishing to reflect upon the fact that the core tenets of Capitalism 1.0 have warranted so little applied attention, by any of the major political parties, over the last two or three decades. Some strange herd mentality has been at work, excluding from the mass media the few voices which have been raised in warning about the potential risks entailed in embracing capitalism of this kind.

The Impact on the Environment

Environmental deregulation has been equally problematic, and it is now similarly inevitable that calls for much stricter regulation can only increase in the future. In Europe, there has been a slowdown in regulatory interventions from the EU, which started in the 1970s and 1980s. These interventions have done more than anything else to help improve both the quality of the physical environment and the quality of life for European citizens. Nonetheless, the EU government just seemed to have lost their regulatory nerve in the face of unprecedented lobbying by big corporations, opting instead for the use of voluntary agreements, or *market measures* instead of what has been endlessly disparaged as "command and control" regulations.

In the United States, back during the administration of George Bush, deregulation was in full swing, as he set out to dismantle the fundamental pillars of environmental regulation, including but not limited to the Clean Air Act, the Clean Water Act, the Endangered Species Act, and so forth. Trump's administration goes on to suggest climate change is a hoax. The consequences of grotesquely inadequate regulation, government after government, administration after administration, are all around us. Thomas Friedman summarizes this admirably in his book titled *Hot, Flat and Crowded*:

> There are no cushions left; there's nowhere to hide; there are no more green fields to dump your garbage into, no more oceans to overfishing, no more endless forests to cut down. We have reached a stage where the effects of our way of life on the earth's climate and biodiversity can no longer be 'externalized' or ignored or confined. Our environmental savings account is empty. It does not pay now or pay ever pay later. It pays now, or there will be no later. There will be no avoiding accountability for the total cost of ownership of what you produce and consume. The days of a 'subprime planet' are over—a planet we could own for no money down, where there were no interest payments until sometime far into the future, and all the real costs were hidden.

As our debts to the banks and others have built up, so have our obligations to nature, at least regarding the unsustainable depletion of natural resources, measured by the loss of top-soil, forests, freshwater, and biodiversity. Everybody knows that liquidating capital assets to fuel current consumption is crazy, but nobody seems to know how to stop it. Judging by the regularity with which politicians trot out today's favorite green clichés, with quotes such as "we do not inherit the world from our parents; we borrow it from our children," you'd think they understood the difference between capital and interest. But they do not.

Some time ago, the Global Footprint Network and the New Economics Foundation launched a new initiative, under the name "Ecological Debt Day," to mark the point in the calendar year at which society exceeded the total volume of resources available to it every year. If we intend to maintain intact our stocks of natural capital, in 2008, their report demonstrated that we went over the limits around September of that year. The direction we are heading is obvious, as are the moral consequences. This kind of deficit consumption is, in effect, draining the capital entitlements of future generations. Given that we never heard a single politician indicate the slightest awareness of this phenomenon, let alone any declared intention of planning to pay back against these ecological debts, we should recognize this for what it is: intergenerational larceny on a staggering scale.

The phenomenon is hardly surprising. When the global population is still increasing by around 70 million people every year, when per capita resource consumption is still increasing every year in all but the poorest countries, and when grown technological productivity can do little more than offset a small part of that combined impact, overshooting our targets is unavoidable. And though no one should ever underestimate the misery caused to hundreds of millions of people by getting into debt and getting stuck in debt, it is our debt to the natural world that matters more than anything else. After Capitalism 1.0 spent billions at trying to recapitalize the banking system, we now hope Capitalism 2.0, sustainable capitalism, can recapitalize the world's environment on an even more heroic scale.

CHAPTER 2

The Need for a More Sustainable System

Overview

Global Sustainable capitalism is an abstract form of capitalism based upon sustainable practices that seek to preserve humanity and the planet while reducing externalities and bearing a resemblance to capitalist economic policy. A capitalistic economy must expand to survive and find new markets to support this expansion. As discussed in Chapter 1, capitalism systems are often thought to be destructive to the environment as well as certain individuals without access to proper representation. However, as argued by Schweickart David (2009), sustainability provides quite the opposite: it implies not only a continuation but a replenishing of resources. Sustainability is often thought to be related to environmentalism, and sustainable capitalism applies sustainable principles to economic governance and social aspects of capitalism as well.

The Importance of Sustainable Capitalism

The importance of sustainable capitalism has been more recently recognized, but the concept is not new. Changes to the current economic model would have substantial social environmental and economic implications and require the efforts of individuals, as well as compliance of local, state, and federal governments. Controversy, as pointed out by Fraker (2013), surrounds the concept as it requires an increase in sustainable practices and a marked decrease in current consumptive behaviors.

This is a concept of capitalism described in Al Gore and David Blood's manifesto for the Generation Investment Management to describe a

long-term political, economic, and social structure, which would miti-
gate current threats to the planet and society. According to their manifesto, sustainable capitalism would integrate the environmental, social,
and governance (ESG) aspects into risk assessment in an attempt to limit
externalities. Most of the ideas they list are related to economic changes
and social issue, but strikingly few are explicitly associated with any
environmental policy change.

We have to be mindful of the physical as well as economic limits to
growth and the capacity of our planet to support our lifestyles. According
to the World Wide Fund for Nature (WWF), we are already using around
1.5 planets to maintain our current consumption patterns, as shown in
Figure 2.1. Our combined ecological footprint, the demand people place
in the natural world, has more than tripled since 1961. Here in the west,
mainly in North America and Europe, the picture is worse still, as we are
already living a three-planet lifestyle. Collectively, we will need two planets by 2030—less than 11 years away.

Taken together, biodiversity loss and an unsustainable footprint
threaten natural systems and human well-being but can also point us
toward actions to reverse current trends. The report calls for action on
strategies to preserve, produce, and consume more wisely and includes
examples of how communities are already making better choices to reduce
footprint and biodiversity loss.

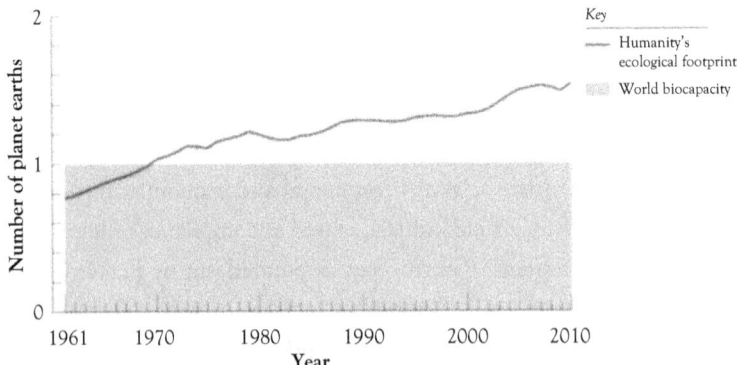

Figure 2.1 The state of the earth: Humanity's ecologic footprint

Source: Global Footprint Network, 2014.

So our current form of capitalism is found wanting on all three counts of performance, including the benefits to our society, environment, and our economies. The call for change is loud, from both within and outside the business world. It is heartening to hear business leaders calling for a new economy, one that is built around triple-bottom-line principles, including shared prosperity and environmental stewardship. But the big question is, what are the alternatives? Also, how do we overcome the dangerous design faults now painfully exposed, to meet the rigorous challenges of our time and enable a business to survive and prosper in the 21st century and beyond, so we can be sure of leaving a positive economic, social, and environmental legacy for the next generation?

Sure, there is some nostalgic debate on whether communism could make a comeback. Marx and Engels wrote in their famous book *The Communist Manifesto* that "what the bourgeoisie, therefore, produces, above all, are its grave-diggers. Its fall and the victory of the proletariat are equally inevitable." Today, almost 200 years after Marx and Engels wrote about grave-diggers, the truth is nearly the exact opposite. The proletariat, far from burying the current version of capitalism, is keeping it on life support, while remaining, overworked and underpaid workers, ostensibly liberated by the most significant socialist revolution in history (China's). Some, like the proverbial examples at Foxconn, have been driven to the brink of suicide to keep those in advanced economies on the West playing with their iPads and iPhones and other similar gadgets. All this while Chinese money is bankrolling an otherwise bankrupt America. This irony is scarcely wasted on leading Marxist thinkers.

According to Jacques Rancière, a French Marxist thinker and professor of philosophy at the University of Paris, "the domination of capitalism globally depends today on the existence of a Chinese Communist party that gives de-localized capitalist enterprises cheap labor to lower prices and deprive workers of the rights of self-organization." Can we hope for a world less absurd and more just than the one we witness today? How ironic is it that global capitalism depends today on the existence of a Chinese communist party?

Some would argue that China has a communist ideology but a capitalist economic system, at least a state capitalism version, which is not a new idea. In the 1990s, there were a lot of state-owned enterprises (SOEs), especially in emerging and frontier economies. The assumption was that, as the economy matured, the government would close or privatize them. China is not alone, as several other countries, including Russia and Brazil, to name a few, have shown no signs of relinquishing the commanding heights, whether in most industries—the world's ten biggest oil and gas companies, measured by reserves, are all state-owned—or principal markets.

State-backed companies account for about 80 percent of the value of China's stock market and 62 percent of Russia's. Although this model still mainly exhibits the same issues that the western model has, even if it allows a longer-term perspective, it is ideologically unlikely to appeal to those with a disposition toward free markets. In the decade since the 2008 global financial crisis, China has increasingly relied on these SOEs to drive its economy. As it faced sweeping unemployment and scrambled to prop up growth after that meltdown, it saw no better option than to pump up its SOE giants with infrastructure, transportation, and real estate projects. The stimulus ended in the early 2010s, but Beijing has continued to turn to SOEs to lead the country's economic transition, raising fears of favoritism among its privately-owned enterprises.

China has sought to strengthen the SOEs with moves to consolidate industries, reduce output capacity, and shrink the amount of debt in the economy. But in doing so, it has strengthened government control over many private businesses and created additional uncertainty and anxiety in both the private sector and society at large. The increasing SOE dominance over several domestic industries and their rapid expansion overseas have put them in the crosshairs of the western world, particularly the United States. Despite those issues, should another economic downturn hit China, the government could once again turn to these giants to keep the economy rolling.

Regardless of government interventions, such as in the United States, the Eurozone, and China, if present climate-change trends continue, the global carbon budget associated with a 2°C increase in average global temperature will be broken in 16 years (while a 1.5°C increase in global average temperature—staying beneath which is the key to long-term stabilization of the climate—will be reached in a decade). Earth System scientists, such as Steffen et al. (2018), warn that the world is now perilously close to a Hothouse Earth, in which catastrophic climate change will be locked in and irreversible. The ecological, social, and economic costs to humanity due to increasing carbon emissions by two percent a year as in recent decades (rising in 2018 by 2.7 percent—3.4 percent in the United States), and failing to meet the minimal three percent annual reductions in emissions currently needed to avoid a catastrophic destabilization of the earth's energy balance are simply incalculable.

Nevertheless, major energy corporations continue to obscure vital information about climate change, promoting and bankrolling climate denialism, while admitting the truth in their internal documents. These corporations are working to accelerate the extraction and production of fossil fuels, including the dirtiest, most greenhouse gas-generating varieties, reaping enormous profits in the process. The melting of the Arctic ice from global warming is seen by capital as a new El Dorado, opening massive additional oil and gas reserves to be exploited without regard to the consequences for the earth's climate. In response to scientific reports on climate change (Gleiser 2016), Exxon Mobil declared that it intends to extract and sell all of the fossil fuel reserves at its disposal. Energy corporations continue to intervene in climate negotiations to ensure that any agreements to limit carbon emissions are defanged. Capitalist countries across the board are putting the accumulation of wealth for a few above combatting climate destabilizations, threatening the very future of humanity.

A Viable Alternative

As argued by Daly (2016), in his work titled *From Uneconomic Growth to a Steady State Economy*, we have now reached a point in the 21st century in which the externalities of Capitalism 1.0 irrational system, such as the costs of war, the depletion of natural resources, the waste of human lives, and the disruption of the planetary environment, now far exceed any future economic benefits that capitalism offers to society as a whole. The accumulation of capital and the amassing of wealth are increasingly occurring at the expense of an irrevocable rift in the social and environmental conditions governing human life on earth

Klaus Schwab, founder and executive chairman of the World Economic Forum (WEF), draws a useful distinction between the ideology of a social market economy, based on individual responsibility on the one hand, and the term capitalism on the other, as a component of an economic system that relates to the capital market. Schwab framed the debate at Davos back in 2016 in such a way that was "not the end of capitalism as an ideology, but the issue of how capitalism's technical components, which have come off the rails, can be reformed."

The argument that capitalism is the culprit for the excesses and mismanagement of the economies around the world is not accurate, and the idea that its imminent demise is near is somewhat exaggerated. We would argue that the capitalist ideology of a free but socially committed and reasonably regulated market economy has never been questioned, not even in Davos. There have been several discussions as to whether capitalism in its present form serves or undermines the free-market economy. A clear distinction needs to be made in this regard between the ideology of a social market economy based on individual responsibility on the one hand and the term capitalism as such on the other.

Over the course of more than 200 years, a range of different interpretations of capitalism has emerged as a reaction to industrialization. In historical terms, the transition from manual trades to machines required an ever-increasing degree of investment, and therefore the provision of capital. In this sense, capitalism is not an ideology as such, but an applied theory of the creation and efficient deployment of resources as a factor of production. In its genuine sense, capitalism is, therefore, the component of an economic system that relates to the capital market, enshrined in the principles of a free market and guaranteed ownership. However, these principles are part of a more comprehensive ideology.

In his excellent book titled *Capitalism as if the Planet Matters (2007)*, Jonathon Porritt takes a pragmatic view that capitalism is the only economic game in town and that all sides must find ways of making free markets deliver a more sustainable future, pretty quickly. Otherwise, the pressures will overwhelm our economies. He rightly generates a sense of urgency.

Unfortunately, in today's parlance, this free-market ideology has been equated with capitalism as a technical component. As a result, it is easy to gain the impression that the free-market economic system founded on individual freedom and, at the same time, social responsibility, is to blame for the excesses of capitalism that has lost its equilibrium, which we would argue is incorrect. What should be at stake in our discussion here is not the end of capitalism as an ideology, but the issue of how capitalism's technical components can be improved.

In short, a call for Capitalism 2.0, one with a vastly upgraded operating system, which also builds on what former U.S. vice-president Al Gore, dubbed as Sustainable Capitalism, is in order. Gore also labeled such a new and improved system a capitalist model that seeks to maximize long-term economic value by reforming markets to address real needs while integrating ESG metrics throughout the decision-making process.

CHAPTER 3

Capitalism 2.0: A More Sustainable System

Overview

Capitalism has great strengths and is fundamentally superior to any other system for organizing economic activity. It is more efficient allocating resources and in matching supply and demand. It is demonstrably effective in wealth creation. It is more congruent with higher levels of freedom and self-governance than any other system. It unlocks a higher fraction of the human potential with ubiquitous, organic incentives that reward demanding work, ingenuity, and innovation. These strengths are why it is at the foundation of every thriving economy.

Capitalism has also proven itself to be adaptable and flexible enough to fit the specific needs of particular countries. Capitalism comes in many forms, from that practiced in the United States to a very different model that has been adopted within communist China. The causes and consequences of these variations are, of course, significant—but the more important fact remains: the mainstream debate is about how to practice capitalism, not whether we should choose between capitalism and some other system.

Yet while the current form of capitalism has proven its superiority, it is nevertheless abundantly clear that some of the ways in which it is now practiced do not incorporate sufficient regard for its impact on people and the planet—and are now posing a number of fundamental challenges that require attention, particularly in a resource-constrained world of 7 billion (soon to be 8–10 billion) people. These include short-termism, over-reliance on gross domestic product (GDP) growth as a primary metric of prosperity, diverting wealth into shadow banking, and financial engineering and away from addressing real needs. These challenges also include rising inequality, increasing volatility in the global financial market, and growing contributions to the climate crisis perpetuated by a resistance to internalize externalities.

In his authoritative *The Age of Extremes: A History of the World 1914–1991*, Marxist historian Eric Hobsbawm, viewing the approach of the 21st century, argued that there were reasons to be concerned that the new century might be even more threatening to humanity than the "age of extremes" that had preceded it, a century that had been punctuated by world wars, imperial conflicts, and economic depressions—and in which humanity was confronted for the first time with the possibility of its own self-annihilation. Yet, looking forward, he concluded, the new century offered even greater dangers.

Hobsbawm observed in 1994 that we live in a world

uprooted and transformed by the titanic economic and the techno-scientific process of the development of capitalism, which has dominated the past two or three centuries. We know, or at least it is reasonable to suppose that it cannot go on ad infinitum. The future cannot be a continuation of the past, and there are signs, both externally, and, as it were, internally, that we have reached a point of a historic crisis. The forces generated by the techno-scientific economy are now significant enough to destroy the environment, that is to say, the material foundations of human life. The structures of human societies themselves, including even some of the social foundations of the capitalist economy, are on the point of being destroyed by the erosion of what we have inherited from the human past. Our world risks both explosion and implosion. It must change.

We do not know where we are going. We only know that history has brought us to this point and—if readers share the argument of this book—why. However, one thing is plain. If humanity is to have a recognizable future, it cannot be by prolonging the past or the present. If we try to build the third millennium on that basis, we shall fail. And the price of failure, that is to say, the alternative to a changed society is gloom.

Hobsbawm left little doubt as to what the principal danger was at present, namely "the theological faith in an economy in which resources were allocated entirely by the totally unrestricted market, under conditions of unlimited competition," carried out by ever-more concentrated corporations. Chief among the dangers of such a system was the likelihood of "irreversible and catastrophic consequences for the natural environment of this planet, including the human race, which is part of it."

Environmental Challenges

The challenges facing the planet today are unprecedented and extraordinary; climate change, water scarcity, poverty, growing inequality of income and wealth, demographic shifts, and a global economy in a state of constant dramatic volatility and flux, to name but a few. While governments and civil society will need to be part of the solution to these challenges, ultimately, it will be companies and investors that will mobilize the capital needed to overcome them.

Before the crisis and since we, and others, have called for a more long-term and responsible form of capitalism, what we call sustainable capitalism seeks to maximize long-term economic value creation. It explicitly integrates environmental, social, and governance (ESG) factors into strategy, the measurement of outputs, and the assessment of both risks and opportunities. Sustainable capitalism is more than corporate social responsibility or impact investing, which are worthwhile endeavors compatible with the precepts of sustainable investing, but narrower in focus. Sustainable capitalism encourages us to generate financial returns in a long-term and responsible manner and calls for internalizing negative externalities through appropriate pricing.

Sustainable capitalism is a framework that seeks to maximize long-term economic value creation by reforming markets to address real needs while considering all costs and integrating ESG metrics into the decision-making process. It applies to the entire investment value chain from entrepreneurial ventures to publicly traded large-cap companies, from investors providing seed capital to those focused on late-stage growth-orientated opportunities, from company employees to CEOs, from activists to policy makers and standard setters. Sustainable capitalism transcends borders, industries, forms of ownership, asset classes, and stakeholders.

Such more sustainable capitalism can provide more than exciting contributions to a variety of emergent patterns related to a fourth industrial revolution, digital disruption platforms that could supplement additional perspective on what happens to conventional measures of economic success locally and nationally and internationally. Likewise, macroeconomics can offer valuable insights related to the understanding of freedoms of movements of labor, capital, and technology or in general, about the effects of liberalization or integration. Some people may not want to rely on such disciplines, outright calling them obsolete, especially some economic gurus, which may lack understanding of such new systematic concepts.

For companies, this means internalizing the business case for sustainability and adapting business models accordingly, with C-level and board support. It means talking openly and candidly about the need to build businesses for the long term and rewarding investors who endorse this approach. Besides, this more responsible approach can be and should be supported by the adoption of integrated reporting. We believe that, in this adapted and enhanced form of sustainable capitalism, it is possible to have a better understanding of the role sustainability can play in economics. Understanding sustainable capitalism is not possible without proper macroeconomic knowledge of some of the underlying processes.

For governments and policy makers, this means understanding that there are severe and ongoing fundamental market failures that threaten not only the future of our companies and investments but also the sustainability of our planet. It means not just focusing on global treaties, government policy, and legal solutions at summits but also understanding and adopting the more immediate changes that can be made to alter incentives and behaviors and partnering with the business to find answers. An ancient prophecy of the classical economy is that every efficient production will meet its demand. People have come gradually to realization for almost a couple of centuries, from the first systematic treatises about the nature of the markets or the stated wealth of the nations. Many people still assume today that, as in classical economists, every supply of goods necessarily meets its demand. Indirectly they think that in that manner that the current system is sustainable. We just have to be practical and efficient and adaptive, and someone is bound to buy the stuff.

Government and policy makers have a pivotal role to play. They must be prepared to go into debt to stimulate the economy when an economy slows down. Fiscal responsibility goes out the window, no matter how conservative the government, when people stop buying—as well it should. Those checks sent to all U.S. taxpayers, courtesy of President Bush and a Democratic congress, aimed at containing the gathering financial storm triggered by the subprime mortgage debacle, should remind us all how vitally a capitalist economy depends on what so many environmentalists and other social critics deride as "consumerism." The problem is not only growth, as healthy capitalism relies not simply on ever-increasing consumption, but on a steady rate of growth. When the growth rate declines, investors pull back. But a constant rate of growth, so essential to healthy capitalism, implies exponential growth, and exponential growth, to anyone with mathematical sensibilities, is alarming. If an economy grows three percent per year, the U.S. average growth rate during the 20th century, consumption doubles every 24 years, which translates into a 16-fold increase in consumption over the course of a century. In reality, we did not have steady growth during the 20th century. On the contrary, we had many ups and downs, such as the Great Depression, fascism, and World War II. Still, the average rate of growth for the century was three percent per year, giving us a 16-fold increase in inflation-adjusted GDP.

For asset owners, this means embracing the long term and sustainability as value-creating tools. In particular, it means recognizing the risks that stranded assets and embracing ways to reshape incentives across the investment value chain. Consultants think tanks, and advisers will be critical in facilitating this change and are urged to adopt similar long-term sustainability-orientated principles.

For investors and asset managers, this means investing in the long term and adopting incentive structures that reward such behavior. It means carefully considering the effect of sustainability factors on the valuation of companies and then changing their mindsets and financial models in response.

For nongovernmental organizations (NGOs), this means clearly defining their role in the economic system. It means developing a better understanding of the motivations of companies and investors and identifying ways to encourage them to change through appropriate methods of impactful engagement. It means drawing attention to unsustainable practices in financial markets and lobbying not just on single issues but for structural changes in the way that the global economy deals with the challenge of sustainability.

For the media, this means challenging companies to do more than just talk about sustainability and holding companies to a high standard when evaluating their actions. It means encouraging the adoption of integrated reporting and celebrating those companies that prove the business case for sustainability. It also means providing a forum for debate to win over the mainstream.

The advocacy of sustainable capitalism is often confronted with arguments on whether integrating sustainability adds value. Yet the question that should be asked of those who are skeptical is why an absence of sustainability does not damage both the company and broader society. Whether there is a formal licensing requirement or not, society ultimately does require, in one way or another, that a company earns the right to operate. When managers do not consider the impact of their decisions on all stakeholders, not just shareholders, we believe that they are putting this license to operate at risk.

The consequence of not maintaining this societal license to operate can be, and often is, damaging to companies in a variety of ways.

- Government and regulatory pressure may restrict corporate freedom to operate.
- Investor flight may increase the corporate's cost of capital.
- Lack of confidence in management may lead to a decline in the valuation of the company and the risk of a takeover.
- Widespread disapproval of a corporate's actions may lead to boycotts or reduced sales and brand degradation.
- Potential business partners and suppliers may be less willing to trade with the company.
- Staff may be unwilling to remain at the corporate and top talent deterred from joining.

Even when social democratic parties come to power in these circumstances, promising to work within the system and create kinder and gentler capitalism, they invariably fall prey to the laws of motion of capitalism in this phase. As Michael Yates writes, in a paper titled *Can the Working Class Change the World?* (2018), in the context of a failed capitalism: "Today, it is impossible to believe that there will be a recovery of even the modest political and economic project that labor unions and political parties once embraced and helped bring to fruition."

What does it mean? It means that classical economists have been wrong to assume that indeterminately, any aggregate supply could meet its demand, globally and locally. Global supply and demand have been officially divorced in the forms of massive financial crisis and stagnation, for at least a third of the last century. The assumption of the possibility of markets to readily solve its dilemmas was refuted by events of the massive crush of capital markets, storming inflations that have turned money into cheap heaps of papers and production capacities into empty warehouses of unsold goods.

What we have readily seen at work through big financial and production and income crisis in a third of the last century could be solely described as the process of overall deconstruction of the money, goods, and factors markets in a systematic manner. It has been the premier sustainability crisis of capitalism. When the global financial crisis hit hard, it squeezed producers and pushed down economic factors' incomes.

Owners of economic factors, such as labor, capital, and resources, further reduced their demand for any goods squashing further production. Social agony and other forms of insecurities swiftly invoked different types of social evils, never at deep sleep, and readily served to stage off what we know as one of the most devastating periods of human history, that of World War II.

As Jørgen Randers, one of the original *Limits to Growth* authors, declares, in 2052—his forecast (in 2012) of the world society 40 years into the future—the "modified capitalism" that will emerge mid-point in this century "will be a system wherein collective well-being is set above the return of the individual." Modified capitalism will be subject to the guidance of "wise government," directed by technocrats while being characterized by "less democracy and less market freedom." Rather than directly facing up to the failures of capitalism—though he projects 40 years of economic stagnation for the major economic powers and continued poverty in the "rest of the world"—Randers sees such questions as mostly irrelevant to his vision of the world in 2052. The dominant reality, he predicts, will be a more efficient and sustainable, if more physically constrained, version of the present-day capitalist society.

Yet, in the barely seven years since his book was written, it is already clear that Randers's predictions were wrong in every respect. The situation confronting the world is qualitatively more severe than it was in 2012, at a time when gradualist, technocratic solutions to climate change still seemed feasible to many, even among those on the left and when the liberal-democratic state appeared perfectly stable. Today, in the context of accelerated climate change, continuing economic stagnation, political upheaval, and growing geopolitical instability, it is clear that the challenges that the world is facing will be both more cataclysmic and epoch-making than progressive ecological modernizers like Randers envisioned. The choices confronting us are now much harder.

Production capacities and therefore repayment capacities of many countries and individuals turned to be either low or vulnerable to swift changes in the environment and got primarily mediated through growth and deepening financial systems and markets. Those who have produced less turned to be less able to attack more investments when the first global crisis hit them, so they lagged further regarding production. Their productive capacities soon become trapped in some forms of the vicious cycle of underdevelopment; the only thing now being added to that is the massive burden of debt(s) on their back.

Now, deterioration of the environment is taking its toll over us. It seriously threatens to undermine everything that we have and what we can do and who we are. We have readily assumed that the environment requires its pace, and we hope that we would readily understand that humans need their speed too since, according to our purpose we are not production machines. Which role belongs to sustainability in the present model of economic growth and under the present business model? Is it time we incorporate sustainability systematically into macroeconomics and development and economic policy theory and practice? This is but a short analytical introduction of some of the features readily available for the macroeconomics of today to ponder about. Now, something of synthetical nature is in order.

First, sustainable development ought to be readily taken as an extension to other macroeconomic goals to be pursued in the new millennia. Second, we need a new framework for the stability and growth of the global economy and global community that is not administrative in manner, but that is not in deep denial of existing problems, as is the case now. Something serious is at stake, and we have to act on it now. We as humans have been able to meet risks and challenges of many sorts, and we can do it again only if we try to improve our fears and suspicions in regards to imminent dangers that we are facing. Third, any new vision of development ought to involve gains and benefits and responsibilities and liabilities of all sides globally. That is the only way toward the new expanding route and cycle of sustainable capitalism and the way out of this deepening crisis, which is a crisis of global demand. Fourth, financial markets cannot help us much on this account to steer things further. We have to do something on the productive side solely, and we have to be more realistic regarding connectedness in general: between all economies globally and between goods markets and factors markets.

Any form of sustainable capitalism has to make markets work more productively and to be more trusted as allocation mechanisms. The same is valid for regulation and global governance. Restructuring on the supply side, namely reforms in the factorial markets and of the goods market, will continue to serve its purpose but with one exception. Their scope and pace ought to be delivered through the freedom of countries to choose the size and extent of their development. It is not reasonable to assume that all can and must develop at the same speed and scope and are able or ought to be pressed to do so.

Therefore, we assume for the sake of a more mature vision of globalization that it will preserve its core values together with sustainability as an alternative vision that, in the long run, could be beneficial for all. I offer here the metaphor of the multilane and multispeed highway. These are several of the features which are critical for the smooth functioning of any highway: lines are separated according to speed and in some cases, to types of vehicles present.

Embracing Environmental, Social, and Governance Metrics

Many corporate leaders, policy makers, and investors remain skeptical about the financial impact of sustainability factors on business performance.

In many cases, this skepticism has blinded them to the risks they presently face by investing in stranded assets and the unsustainable companies that maintain them. Stranded assets are those that would be unprofitable under specific scenarios, which include the enforcement of a fair price on carbon and water, or improved regulation of labor standards in emerging and frontier economies. Only limited work has been done to date to quantify the potential impact these sorts of changes would have on the value of companies, but one such piece by the Carbon Tracker Initiative (CTI) provides new insights into the likely impact of stranded assets.

Carbon Tracker Initiative

According to CTI reports, just using the fossil fuel reserves of the top 100 coal, oil, and gas companies over the next 40 years would emit enough carbon to raise global warming by more than 2°C.[1] An increase of 2°C in global temperature would, in the view of many scientists, bring catastrophic risks to civilization. These include the risk of multimeter sea-level increases in this century (with large numbers of "climate refugees" forced to leave their ancestral homes); deepening droughts in densely populated areas and crucial agricultural breadbaskets; increased frequency and severity of costly and dangerous extreme weather events such as the 2010 floods in Pakistan, Australia, Colombia, and elsewhere; accelerating loss of plant and animal species; and widespread health risks. Indeed, some scientific leaders, such as NASA's James Hansen, point out that the "two-degree" threshold is essentially a political construct and does not represent a scientific conclusion about what would be a "safe" level of global average temperature increase. These environmental disasters directly link back to

---

[1] Carbon Tracker Initiative, Unburnable Carbon – Are the World's Financial Markets Carrying a Carbon Bubble? 2011. http://carbontracker.org/carbonbubble.

the ability of businesses to sustain long-term profitability as the implications of a temperature increase exceeding 2°C would create mass global upheaval, uprooting people through forced migration, inevitably causing disruption in companies and instability in financial markets, showcasing the looming negative implications if the risks related to stranded assets are not identified and mitigated.

Some sell-side analysts criticized the CTI analysis because it is hard to build the implications of their report into a valuation model and that there is significant policy uncertainty over how climate-change regulation will develop. These are valid practical concerns but, in many ways, simply serve to confirm the underlying problem: current valuations are inaccurate and beg a solution similar to the "value at risk" (VAR) concept used by mainstream traders, to show an adjusted value for assets after accounting for climate change.

Incremental change will only result in our society becoming less unsustainable, rather than sustainable. As such, an attitudinal framework like the one now in place, which all too frequently stalls change and innovation related to identifying and incorporating risks from stranded assets, must be dismantled.

We encourage working with academics and financial professionals to quantify the impact of stranded assets and the subsequent implications for assessing investment opportunities until a fair price on externalities forces a change in valuation methodologies. Our goal is to establish the financial materiality of sustainability through empirical evidence. And through this analysis, we hope to provoke a more comprehensive discussion about the need for investors, in particular, those with long-term liabilities, to fundamentally reassess their investment thesis relating to externalities rather than merely hedging against them.

Providing Ongoing Support for a Sustainable Capitalism

As we advocate for sustainable capitalism, we are often challenged to spell out why sustainability adds value. Yet the question that should be asked instead is, why does an absence of sustainability not damage companies, investors, and society at large? From BP and ExxonMobil to Lehman Brothers and AIG, there is a long list of examples proving that it does. Moreover, companies and investors that integrate sustainability into their business practices are finding that it enhances profitability over the longer term.

Experience and research show that embracing sustainable capitalism yields four kinds of significant benefits for companies:

1. Developing sustainable products and services can increase a company's profits, enhance its brand, and improve its competitive positioning, as the market increasingly rewards this behavior.
2. Sustainable capitalism can also help companies save money by reducing waste and increasing energy efficiency in the supply chain and by improving human-capital practices so that retention rates rise and the costs of training new employees decline.
3. Focusing on ESG metrics allows companies to achieve higher compliance standards and better manage risk since they have a more holistic understanding of the material issues affecting their business.
4. Researchers (including Rob Bauer and Daniel Hann of Maastricht University, and Beiting Cheng, Ioannis Ioannou, and George Serafeim of Harvard) have found that sustainable businesses realize financial benefits such as lower cost of debt and lower capital constraints.

Sustainable capitalism is also important for investors. Serafeim and his colleague Robert G. Eccles have shown that sustainable companies outperform their unsustainable peers in the long term. Therefore, investors who identify companies that embed sustainability into their strategies can earn substantial returns while experiencing low volatility.

We believe that there are several broader ideas circulating among research circles, the World Economic Forum, the United Nations, and many other think tanks around the globe. This book is more of a conceptual work supporting sustainable capitalism than a series of practical recommendations to tackle the problem, which we believe will take much more effort and integrated science throughout the world. But there are five broader ideas that merit ongoing support and attention:

1. **Sustainable capitalism as a fiduciary issue:** While the business case for sustainable capitalism is clear, several corporate executives and investment funds continue to be unsure about whether sustain-

able capitalism is a fiduciary issue. It is clear that the broad trend is toward the acceptance of sustainable capitalism factors as a legitimate consideration by the board of directors and even, increasingly, as an essential consideration. Intel is a great example, as back in 2010, the company made sustainability a fiduciary duty by amending its corporate charter to include mandatory reporting on "corporate responsibility and sustainability performance."

2. **Creation of advisory services for sustainable asset management:** The investment consultancy industry provides essential advice to corporate governance, government, and investment funds both on the qualities of particular asset managers and on asset allocation strategies. While many of the leading investment consultancies have invested in developing sustainable investment teams and are conducting significant research in the area, in most cases sustainability has not yet penetrated mainstream investment consulting advice. Although many mainstream investment funds are not currently demanding information about sustainability issues from their investment consultants, that failure does not change the affirmative duty that investment consultants have to inform clients of the financial materiality of sustainability. The range of ways that sustainability can be incorporated into investing is extensive, but this makes it even more critical that investment consultants are able to distinguish between the approaches taken by fund managers and to understand the implications that this has on their performance and impact on sustainability.

3. **Expansion of the range and depth of sustainable investment products:** There is an increasing number of sustainable investment products from both mainstream and boutique investors. Mainstreaming sustainable capitalism will require products from a range of asset classes and will require that the best products reach scale. We would recommend the scaling of products beyond the traditional focus of public equity. But given the lack of track records for many new products, it will be essential for intermediaries and others to consider how to position such products effectively.

4. **Reconsider the appropriate definition of growth beyond GDP:** Rampant hyperconsumption fueled by easy access to credit has not only destroyed value in the global economy but also done significant

harm to the environment—and yet is still counted as a positive contribution to "progress," as measured by GDP growth. As part of the transition to sustainable capitalism, the previously assumed metric for success focused on maximum growth, must be reconsidered in the context of consumption, income distribution, and quality-of-life indicators. The quality, not merely the quantity, of growth, should be valued. By ignoring externalities, GDP is too narrow a definition of growth. More needs to be done to build consensus around what metrics should be measured to track sustainable growth at both the country and corporate level. More also should be done subsequently to integrate the new definition of progress into political and business decision making.

5. **Integrate sustainability into business education at all levels:** Sustainable capitalism will require the incorporation of sustainability into the education and training of current and future managers, consultants, executives, and investors. The continuing education of current practitioners should include:

- Raising awareness among corporate executives, business strategists, policy makers, and asset managers of the importance of sustainable investing and providing information on how to launch ESG products across asset classes;
- Working with investor-relations teams and investment consultants who can encourage adoption by their respective investor base of long-term sustainability-orientated thinking, and
- Training corporate boards on how to integrate sustainability into their duties and strategic planning for companies. To educate future leaders, undergraduate and business school courses should integrate sustainability across a range of disciplines. This is a topic for which we devote two chapters later in this book.

The answers to the crises before us are both social and ecological. They require the rational regulation of the metabolism between human beings and nature under the control of associated humanity—regenerating and maintaining the flows, cycles, and other vital processes of healthy, local, regional, and global ecosystems (and species habitats)—in accord with the needs of the entire chain of human generations. The mainsprings of human action throughout history lie in the drive for human freedom and the struggle to master our relation to the world. The first of these ultimately demands equality and community; the other, human development, and sustainability. It is on these struggles for collective advancement that we must ultimately rely on if humanity is to have a future at all.

The Economics of Sustainable Development

On a finite planet, endless economic growth is impossible. There is also plenty of evidence that in the advanced economies, a continued increase in GDP does not increase happiness. Back in 1930 the economist John Maynard Keynes predicted that growth would end within a century—but he was unclear whether postgrowth capitalism was really possible. Today, mainstream economic thinking still considers growth to be a vital policy objective—essential to the health of a capitalist economy. There remains a concern that ultimately, a capitalist economy will collapse without growth.

Previous studies on "postgrowth economics" have tended to search for an elusive sweet spot where the economy would be steady and robust enough to cope with all shocks. But theorizing along those lines fails to address the question of whether an end to growth would, in general, make an economy more or less stable.

In researching for this book, Dr. Svigir developed a somewhat novel mathematical macroeconomic model, making use of American economist Hyman Minsky's theory of financial instability. He argued that financial crises are to be expected in capitalist systems because periods of economic prosperity encourage borrowers and lenders to be progressively more reckless. Minsky's work was somewhat overlooked before the 2008 crash but has received increased attention since.

The model included a banking sector that charges businesses interest on loans. That way, it could address the concern that this crucial feature of capitalism might in itself create a need for growth. While other aspects of finance could be reformed for a postgrowth economy, it is hard to imagine capitalism without debt and interest. The model also included an underlying labor market, with dynamic wages. The analysis becoming a reality on a sophisticated systems dynamics approach. Simple assumptions combine to create a nonlinear model of an economy whose behavior is diverse and unpredictable. This approach is essential for a full understanding of the fluctuations, cycles—and occasional crises—that real economies go through. In looking at results, we were interested in whether or not there was runaway explosive behavior. In a stable scenario, the growth of GDP fluctuated around the increase in productivity. But in an unstable situation, the fluctuations would get bigger and bigger, until a collapse occurred.

Far more important for stability was debt behavior. In line with Minsky's theory, the more rapidly businesses try to change their level of debt in response to fluctuations, the more likely there is to be a crisis. The results showed that businesses should not take on new debt when there is an economic upswing, nor should they engage in any panic-induced debt payoff during a temporary downswing. The results even suggested that low debt volatility was more important for stability than the overall level of debt. There are, of course, reforms that would have to be made to the global financial system. Dr. Svigir found that an end to growth reduces profits for business owners. Therefore, if it remains relatively easy for money to flow across borders, then investors might abandon a postgrowth country for a fast-growing developing country. Also, businesses are beholden to shareholders keen on growth as a means of rapid profit accumulation.

It may be that environmentalists trying to protect the Earth's resources do not have the power themselves to curb the excesses of capitalism. However, growth has slowed in advanced economies, as discussed earlier, and as some mainstream commentators and economists are now predicting a transition to a postgrowth era, whatever our environmental policy—which means the study of postgrowth economics is a field which itself will grow.

Sustainable Development

As a sustainable development reference point, we have considered a report written by James Robertson for the European Commission in 1997, published in 1999, entitled "New Economics of Sustainable Development." Most of the references we adopted in this book related to sustainable development economics have been taken from this source. Robertson had written this report at a time when the euro was on the verge of becoming a reality, and the EU was, more than ever, affected by the need to offer its citizens a kind of development which could meet their needs of the present, but without compromising the economic capacity of future generations to meet theirs.

Almost 20 years later, such an experiment has confirmed or refuted some of the expectations placed on the EU's economy and its economic policy making, starting with the impact it has had on the average lives of the European people, its businesses, and overall public well-being. When the EU Commission's Forward Studies Unit tasked Robertson to attempt to synthesize the idea of sustainable development economics, such thought was best known as alternative economics for sustainable development. As such, it was implied that by being an *alternative* it had no ambition to be in line or become mainstream or one of the mainstream versions of economics for the EU block, or the global economy for that matter.

Notwithstanding, it has become a central point of this research to attempt to organize a conversation around this topic, discussing the basic postulates of economics of sustainable development with mainstream economics, not only from the perspective of predominant neo-classical economic theory of the 20th century, but also from a variety of other mainstream popular economic stances advocated by Keynesian economics, monetary economics, theory of game economics, behavioral approaches, and institutional economics.

Note, our usage of the term *mainstream* here refers to the mixture of these approaches, and when needed, we highlight the differences and similarities of these models. In this process, we try to use plain and simple language, avoiding technical jargon, so that noneconomist readers can appreciate the ideas we propose. Of course, there is a risk in the simplification of economics concepts, but we believe that passing our message of sustainable capitalism forward is of greater importance than attempting to enrich economic theory or offer any significant scientific contribution.

Robertson's starting reference point is

... Conventional economic progress fails to meet the needs of many millions of people today and compromises the ability of future generations to meet their needs. The new economics reflects the growing worldwide demand for new ways of economic life and thought that would conserve the environment and its resources and empower people to meet their own needs and the needs of others.

The principles and economic focus of sustainable development according to Robertson's report include:

1. Systematic empowerment of people (as opposed to making and keeping them dependent), as the basis for people-centered development;
2. Systematic conservation of resources and environment, as the basis for environmentally sustainable development;
3. An evolution from a "wealth of nations" model of economic life to a one-world model, and from today's international economy to an ecologically sustainable, decentralizing, multilevel one-world economic system;
4. Restoration of political and ethical factors to a central place in economic life and thought;
5. Respect for qualitative values, not just quantitative values; respect for feminine values, not just masculine ones.

According to Robertson, the following features of the new economics underline its direct relevance to policy making:

- It is normative, focusing on action to create a better future for people and the environment.
- It is based on a realistic view of human nature, recognizing that people are both altruistic and selfish, cooperative, and competitive.
- It recognizes that evolving the economic system to reward activities that are socially and environmentally benign (and not the reverse, as at present) will make socially and environmentally responsible choices the more accessible choices for people and organizations.
- It is about transforming today's economic life and thought, shaping a new mainstream for the future, not just about

promoting secondary alternatives coexisting with today's mainstream.

- It is dynamic and developmental, working for changes in the direction of progress, not to a blueprint for a final destination.
- Its approach is systemic and synergistic. It looks for "framework" policies that will promote sustainable development in every field, and it recognizes that more sustainable development in one area will be closely linked with sustainable development in every other.
- It is critical and constructive, based on the recognition that effective opposition to conventional economic development and thought is a necessary part of the transformation, but those constructive alternatives must also be proposed.
- It recognizes the need to combine short-term with long-term change. Short-term policy changes to meet current mainstream policy objectives should be such as will help to open the way to new policy objectives and more fundamental changes in the longer term.

Actually, most of these ideas have already been part of the mainstream economics but perhaps not so much of the main mainstream economics; but normative approach, critical appraisal, dissolution of short term, and dynamic versus static approach.

Since human agency as emphasized by the postulates of the economics of sustainable development is ambivalent, one should not expect that all behavior will be immediately changed. Proper policies need to be developed with adequate sustainability support. According to the Robertson report presented to EU's stakeholders almost 20 years ago, there are several projects that have been defined as an alternative, including

- Restructuring the tax system in favor of environmentally benign development and higher levels of employment and useful work.
- The introduction of a citizen's income paid unconditionally to all citizens in place of many existing social welfare benefits.

- Termination of subsidies and other public expenditure programs that encourage unsustainable development.
- Introduction of public purchasing policies that encourage contractors to adopt sustainable practices.
- Development of more self-reliant local economies, involving (among other things) support for local banking and financial institutions.
- Local means of exchange (local "currencies"), local shops, and easier access for local people to local "means of production."
- Development of indicators to measure economic, social, and environmental performance and progress.
- Development of accounting, auditing, and reporting procedures (and other accreditation procedures) to establish the sustainability performance of businesses and other organizations.
- Demand reduction policies (e.g., for transport and energy), and the need to consider their implications.
- Changes in the existing international trading regime to encourage sustainable forms of trade.
- Systematic reviews should be carried out and published on the possibilities for reorientating public spending programs, with the aim of preventing and reducing environmental and social problems before the event, rather than concentrating on trying to clean up and remedy their effects afterward.
- As the damaging nature of the money and finance system becomes more apparent, a postmodern perspective on money, appropriate to the Information Age, is beginning to come into focus.

In that respect economics of sustainable development proposes:

- Multiple and multilevel currency systems;
- Mitigating the unsustainable effects of interest and debt;
- Deregulating currencies and quasi-currencies;
- Adoption of electronic money;

- The need to apply sustainability accounting, auditing, and accreditation procedures to financial institutions; and the role of green and social investment, and the role of local banking and microcredit institutions, in the shift to sustainability making.

CHAPTER 4

Fostering a Sustainable Development

Overview

According to the Brundtland Commission (WECD 1987), sustainable development meets the needs of the present without compromising the ability of the future generation to meet their own needs. It includes a sustainable dimension of social, economic, and environmental (Kiron et al. 2012) or people, planet, and profit (Ten Bos and Bevan 2011) dimension. Brundtland Commission goes further in explaining that meeting essential needs requires not only a new era of economic growth for nations in which the majority are poor but an assurance that those poor get their fair share of the resources required to sustain that growth. Such equity would be aided by a political system that secures effective citizens' participation in decision making and by greater democracy in international decision making (WCED 1987).

Environmental Strategies for Sustainability

In 1983, the World Commission for Environment and Development was formulated in order to propose long-term environmental strategies for achieving sustainable development by the year 2000. It emphasized several of the issues related to the future sustainability path. It aimed toward greater cooperation among developing countries and among countries at a different level of economic and social development leading to the achievement of common and mutually supportive objectives that take account of the interrelationships between people, resources, environment, and development.

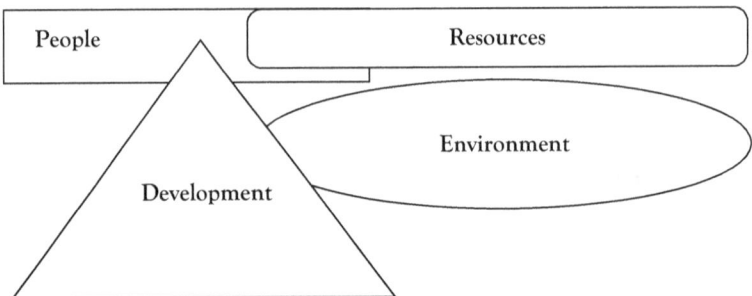

Figure 4.1 Sustainable capitalism as an interrelationship's reality

We have taken several of the key UN sustainable development documents to map their systemic sustainability approach describing them as features of sustainable capitalism in the making. Because of the precision and many times of ingenuity of these documents and elaborated ideas related to sustainable economics and business model, we have attempted to use verbatim formulations, only occasionally making interventions complementing it with supplementary statistics that we have analyzed relating to a variety of subjects. The primary purpose of this approach is to highlight the critical sustainable capitalism features, as depicted in Figure 4.1, of neglected reality, of the interconnectivity of the social, environmental, and economic elements of development.

The so-called global civilization-related innovation that the UN has introduced by its "first working body commission" elaboration of the sustainability agenda was that environmental issues, together with development issues, have been defined as universal rights. Not just as potential but as an economic path that is interrelated to overall sustainability rights trajectories. What we considered as crucial in this respect is that UN, even before almost four decades, appealed to citizens' groups, nongovernmental organizations, educational institutions, and scientific community, calling them all into creating a momentum of public awareness and political change for the global suitability agenda.

Both realities, the scope and the approach to sustainability agenda, are still valid and urgent unfinished missions. Likewise, within this recommendation, we see a mandate and potential mission of business schools to become one of the main stakeholders in proposing and championing sustainable capitalism but also in contributing through its educational missions to its elaboration providing educational modules for global sustainable capitalism stakeholders. It is vital to emphasize that the sustainability agenda cannot be defined and prescribed only for those who can sort off "afford it." UN was quite elaborate even at the start of global sustainability campaign that economic and social development must be defined in terms of sustainability in and of all countries—developed or developing, market-oriented or centrally planned.

The way we use the term sustainable capitalism is only as a definition of a predominantly global economic system, but it is quite clear that sustainability features have to correspond to all socioeconomic systems, as discussed in earlier chapters. Inevitably sustainable development defined in such a systemic manner involves the progressive transformation of economy and society. Physical sustainability, as UN documents claim, cannot be secured unless development policies pay attention to such considerations as changes in access to resources and the distribution of costs and benefits of economics or business model to all.

Transforming Economies and Societies

Even the narrow notion of physical sustainability implies a concern for social equity between generations, a matter that must logically be extended

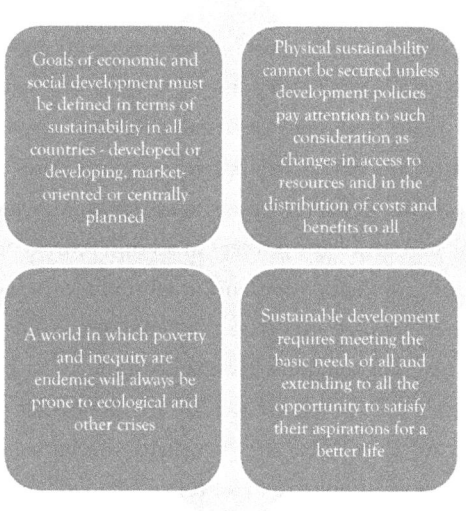

Figure 4.2 Sustainable capitalism progressively transforms the economy and society

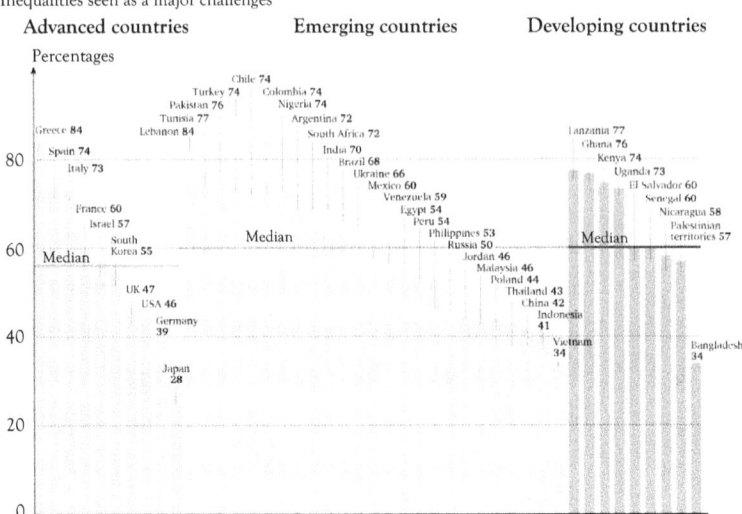

Figure 4.3 Sustainable capitalism reduces the widening gap between rich and poor

Source: Spring 2014 Global Attitudes survey, Pew Research Center

to equity within each generation. This means greening of the existing mainstream socioeconomic system would not do. Sustainable capitalism embedded in sustainable development is, therefore, as depicted in Figure 4.2, only possible as the progressive transformation of the entire system that reevaluates the importance of the social and natural capital besides creating value-added and cumulated value of financial capital.

One of the main postulates of sustainable capitalism in the making is that inequalities are always related to ecological crises and vice versa. Sustainable capitalism, therefore, continues and is even strengthening its mission to challenge and fight poverty in all of its forms but also in challenging the existing systemic problems of all that are excluded or that are left behind. Three decades after its first documents on sustainability UN has prepared a new sustainability agenda document that has pronounced this global sustainable mission through the following statements: an action plan for people, planet, and prosperity, strengthening of the universal peace, eradicating poverty in all forms by involving transformative steps toward the sustainable and resilient path that leaves no one behind.

The vision brought forward is the world free of hunger, poverty, disease, fear, and violence, achieving universal literacy, equitable universal access to education, health, and social protection, right to drinking water, improved hygiene, and sanitation, safe human habitat, and universal access to affordable, reliable, and sustainable energy. Figure 4.3 depicts inequalities among advanced, emerging, and frontier (developing) economies.

Widening Global Inequality

The UN warned about the widening gap between rich and poor almost four decades ago, but even more importantly, the UN has approached this inequality as the planet's main "environmental" problem being also its main development-related problem. A world where poverty is endemic, the UN emphasizes, will always be prone to ecological and other disasters. Emerging countries are forced to overexploit environmental resources for the sake of the export of resources, often to pay for their excessive debts. Environment gets rapidly degraded in all manners (including desertification, destroying of forests, acid precipitation of soil, global warming, greenhouse effect, shifting agricultural production areas, raising of the sea level and flooding of the coastal cities, depletion of ozone shield, toxic substances in food chains and underground waters) so the need for sustainable capitalism comes from the growing realization that it is impossible to separate economic development from environmental issues.

An increase in poverty and unemployment have increased the pressure on environmental resources, and many governments struggling with their fiscal potential, unfortunately, have cut back efforts to protect the environment, not bringing ecological considerations into development planning. In that respect, again poor are in a particularly delicate situation since they require most environment-related intervention yet have least resource for the financing of these activities, particularly on a more continuous basis. The problem of misconduct that comes from the separation of development from environmental protection arises out of artificial compartmentalization of human activities. The question of artificial compartmentalization of human activities (involving separation between environment, economics, and social issues) is present within nations and within sectors in both developed and developing countries. That is why not much has been done on the sustainability agenda in a systemic manner.

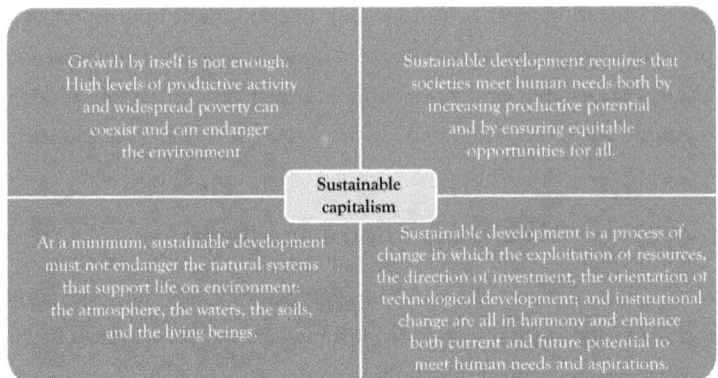

Figure 4.4 Sustainable capitalism challenges global ecological crisis by addressing and eradicating poverty and inequality and resultant depletion of natural resources

Globally this failure is related to all activities that aspired to localize and "fix" sustainability-related problems at national or sectoral levels; sustainable capitalism could not be confined as such, as depicted in Figure 4.4. Notably, a sharp increase of economic interdependence of countries in the course of economic globalization is followed by an accelerated ecological interdependence among nations. Degradation of nature cannot be localized. Growth of population and industrial growth create pressure on natural resources, especially on those poorest. Degradation of environment and development of the poorest have been described by UN as one of the factors that will prompt higher and uncontrolled migrations from the most impoverished countries toward most developed countries (this became obvious even several decades ago).

As we have already pointed out previously UN sustainability agenda places at the center a principle stating that the world in which poverty and inequality are endemic will always be prone to ecological and other crises. Sustainable development requires, in terms of challenging poverty and inequality, meeting the basic needs of all and extending to all the opportunity to satisfy their aspirations for a better life. In that sense, we do not speak only of redistributive reality but also wider global mission and vision of sustainable capitalism. A couple of decades ago the movement concerned with principles and practice of sustainable production and consumption was started.

The living standards that go beyond the essential minimum are sustainable only if consumption standards everywhere have regard for long-term sustainability. UN sustainability agenda claims that the perceived needs of humanity, groups, and individuals are socially and culturally determined. During that understanding and promotion of sustainable capitalism, we will require the development of values that encourage consumption standards that are ecologically possible and to which all can reasonably aspire. UN, in the course of its sustainability mission, has rightfully asserted that meeting of essential needs depends in part on achieving full growth potential, and sustainable development clearly requires economic growth in places where such needs are not being met. But growth by itself is not enough. High levels of productive activity and widespread poverty can coexist and can endanger the environment. Hence sustainable capitalism requires that societies meet human needs both by increasing productive potential and by ensuring equitable opportunities for all.

Currently, despite the overwhelming body of optimistic rhetoric, that is not the case. At the same time, sustainable capitalism can only be pursued if demographic developments are in harmony with the changing productive potential of the ecosystem. UN has recognized that not only poverty and environmental degradation but also population growth is inextricably related and that none of these fundamental problems can be successfully addressed in isolation. In general, renewable resources like forests and fish stocks need not be depleted provided the rate of use is within the limits of regeneration and natural growth. That is a response to criticism stating that sustainable capitalism is only about the limitation and conservation of natural resources not considering human development and survival-related activities. It is obvious that problems are due to the excessive level of exploitation of human and natural resources. As depicted in Figure 4.5, sustainable capitalism moves away from exploitations of human and natural capital in scale and scope and moves toward the more natural scope of their regeneration. Renewable resources are parts of a complex and interlinked ecosystem, and maximum sustainable yield must be defined after considering systemwide effects of exploitation.

Figure 4.5 also shows that global growth after great financial crises that occurred in 2008 and the worldwide decline of 2009 have turned

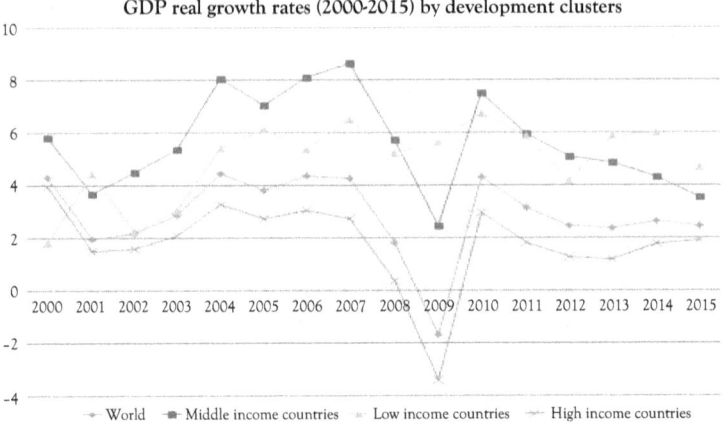

Figure 4.5 Sustainable inclusive capitalism challenges inequalities of all kinds

Source: Authors' calculations according to the World Bank database

into a continuance of global growth of developed countries only. After the global financial crisis world has primarily moved away from less developed countries and both least developed and middle-income economy countries, which cumulatively slowed the global growth prospects. Only most developed countries continued to show growth potential which is the crucial argument for the statement that other things being equal we may assume that world again would only increase the level of the global economic product, but it would not reduce the existing economic, social, and environmental levels of inequalities.

Again, less, and least developed countries would be forced to overexploit their resources: human and nature. UN had, in its first report in the mid-1980s of the last centuries warned that many problems arise from inequalities in access to resources. An inequitable land ownership structure can lead to overexploitation of resources in the smallest holdings, with harmful effects on both environment and development. Internationally, monopolistic control over resources can drive those who do not share them with excessive exploitation of limited resources. The differing capacities of exploiters to commandeer "free" goods—locally, nationally, and internationally—are another manifestation of unequal access to resources. "Losers" in environment/development conflicts include those who suffer more than their fair share of the health, property, and ecosystem damage costs of pollution.

In this sense, inequality and equality are related to systemic access and systemic inability to access resources in a more equitable manner. When a system approaches ecological limits, inequalities sharpen. When a watershed deteriorates, poor farmers suffer more because they cannot afford the same antierosion measures as more prosperous farmers. When urban air quality declines, the poor, in their more vulnerable areas, suffer more health damage than the rich, who usually live in more pristine neighborhoods. When mineral resources become depleted, late-comers to the industrialization process lose the benefits of low-cost supplies. Hence, our inability to promote the common interest in sustainable development is often a product of the relative neglect of economic and social justice within and amongst nations. That is why the notion of social and environmental justice becomes one of the critical features of sustainable capitalism in the making.

Almost three decades after its "Our Common World Report," the UN has, in the course of monitoring its so-called global sustainability goals expanded this element related to inequality in the sense that it now speaks of inclusive sustainable development versus exclusive ones to leave many behind. This new notion of inclusiveness (social, economic, political, and cultural) is related to empowerment behind the principle of nondiscrimination. It refers to the need to include everyone in societal processes and conveys the notion that people should not only be allowed to thrive but also have a voice and effective opportunities.

Equality, as a concept, has traditionally been related to equality of outcomes and equality of opportunities. Inequality of opportunities refers to cases where different people or sections of society do not have the same opportunity to participate in society and to flourish. This can be the result of explicit and implicit barriers to specific sections of the population, such as discrimination in the law, in custom, and in practice, which limits access to opportunities for certain groups in society. Equality can also be seen in a political sense and related to empowerment. Equality, in that sense, refers to giving different people and sections of equal society voice and equal opportunities in political and social institutions and more control over their lives.

The UN identifies the following international equality and inclusion policy responses: measures related to official development assistance and other financial means; commitments to increase or support investment in specific sectors, with focus on developing countries, for example, agriculture, medicines, and infrastructure; international cooperation and technical assistance; actions on trade; promoting the rule of law at the international level; enhancing collaboration on and access to science, technology, and innovation.

National equality and inclusion policy responses, on the other hand, are aimed at ensuring universal and equal access to basic services; ensuring access to food for all, and end malnutrition; achieving and sustaining income growth of the bottom 40 percent of the population at a rate higher than the national average; doubling agricultural productivity of small-scale food producers, putting in place social protection systems and policies; building the resilience of the poor and vulnerable allowing them access to employment; and expanding infrastructure with a focus on affordable and equitable access for all.

Ending discrimination policy responses are aimed at empowering and promoting the social, economic, and political inclusion of all; ending all forms of discrimination against women and girls; eliminating violence against women and girls; ending abuse, exploitation, trafficking, and all forms of violence against and torture of children; recognizing unpaid care and domestic work; equal access to technical, vocational, and tertiary education; and equal pay for work of equal value, eliminating discriminatory laws, policies, and practices and promoting and enforcing appropriate legislation, policies, and action in this regard; promoting the rule of law and ensuring equal access to justice for all; protecting fundamental freedoms; eradicating forced labor, including the worst forms of child labor, human trafficking; protecting labor rights, and providing legal identity for all. The following are the opportunities for empowerment and enhancing capabilities policy response:

- Access to sexual and reproductive healthcare services
- Enhancing access to markets and financial services for households and SMEs
- Ensuring responsive, inclusive, participatory, and representative decision making

- Ensuring women's full and effective participation and equal opportunities for leadership at all levels of decision making in political, economic, and public life
- Fiscal, wage policies aiming to progressively achieve greater equality; use of enabling technology, in particular, information and communications technology
- Full and productive employment and decent work
- Increase in skills for employment and entrepreneurship, ensuring equal access to economic resources
- Literacy and numeracy
- Policies that support productive activities, decent job creation, entrepreneurship, creativity, and innovation
- Provision of public services and infrastructure
- Universal access to sexual and reproductive health and reproductive rights
- Universal primary and secondary education

As depicted in Figure 4.6, sustainable capitalism must not endanger the natural systems that support life on the environment, the atmosphere, the waters, the soils, and the living beings.

Settled agriculture, the diversion of watercourses, the extraction of minerals, the emission of heat and harmful gases in to the atmosphere, commercial forests, and genetic manipulation are all examples of human

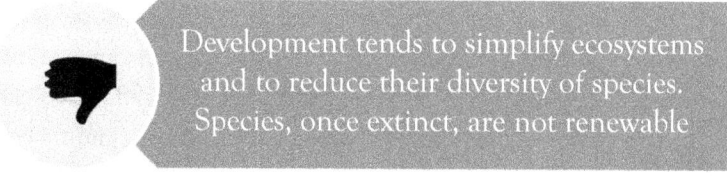

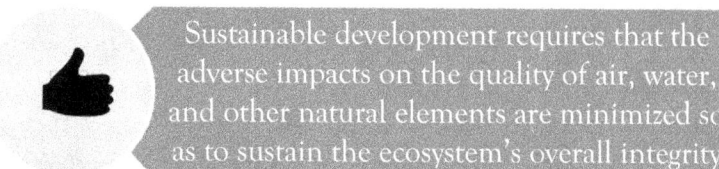

Figure 4.6 Sustainable capitalism must not endanger the natural habitats

intervention in natural systems during the course of development. At a minimum, sustainable capitalism must not endanger the natural systems that support life on the environment. With minerals and fossil fuels, the rate of depletion and the emphasis on recycling and economy of use should be calibrated to ensure that the resource does not run out before acceptable substitutes are available. Sustainable capitalism requires that the rate of depletion of nonrenewable resources should foreclose as few future options as possible. Development tends to simplify ecosystems and to reduce their diversity of species. And species, once extinct, are not renewable.

The loss of plant and animal species can limit the options of future generations, so sustainable capitalism requires the conservation of plant and animal species. The so-called free goods like air and water are also resources. The raw materials and energy of production processes are only partly converted to useful products. The rest comes out as wastes. Sustainable capitalism requires that the adverse impacts on the quality of air, water, and other natural elements are minimized to sustain the ecosystem's overall integrity. In essence, sustainable capitalism is a process of change in which the exploitation of resources, the direction of investments, the orientation of technological development, and institutional change are all in harmony and enhance both current and future potential to meet human needs and aspirations.

The principal global development challenge, as emphasized by UN, is to meet the needs and aspirations of an expanding developing world population. The most basic of all requirements is for a livelihood, that is, employment. The pace and pattern of economic development have to generate sustainable work opportunities on this scale and at a level of productivity that would enable poor households to meet minimum consumption standards. Another priority is food production, but increased food production should not be based on ecologically unsound production policies and compromise long-term prospects for food security. Sustainable development can be pursued more easily when population size is stabilized at a level consistent with the productive capacity of the ecosystem. In that sense three decades ago, this challenge has been identified in the phenomenon of growing population countries struggling with poverty and hunger and their problems related to how to quickly lower population growth rates, especially in regions such as Africa, where these rates are increasing. Developing countries in that respect will have to promote direct measures to reduce fertility to avoid going radically beyond the productive potential to support their populations.

Sustainable capitalism, on the other hand, ought to be related to the development of smaller urban centers reducing the pressures in large cities. Solving the impending urban crisis will require the promotion of self-help housing and urban services by and for the poor, and a more positive approach to the role of the informal sector, supported by enough funds for water supply, sanitation, and other services. If needs are to be met on a sustainable basis, the environment's natural resource base must be conserved and enhanced.

Significant changes in policies will be needed to cope with the industrial world's current elevated levels of consumption and consumption required to meet minimum standards in developing countries in the context of expected population growth. Land use in agriculture and forestry must be based on a scientific assessment of land capacity, and the annual depletion of topsoil, fish stock, or forest resources must not exceed the rate of regeneration. Short-sighted, short-term improvements in productivity can create different forms of ecological stress, such as the loss of genetic diversity in standing crops, salinization, and alkalization of irrigated lands, nitrate pollution of groundwater, and pesticide residues in food. Ecologically more benign alternatives are available. Future increases in productivity, in both developed and developing countries, should be based on better controlled application of water and agrochemicals, as well as on more extensive use of organic manures and nonchemical means of pest control.

Finally, the ultimate limits to global development are determined by the availability of energy resources and by the biosphere's capacity to absorb the by-products of energy use. These energy limits may be approached far sooner than the restrictions imposed by other material resources. First, there are the supply problems: the depletion of oil reserves, the excessive cost and environmental impact of coal mining, and the hazards of nuclear technology. Second, there are emission problems, most notably acid pollution and carbon dioxide build-up leading to global warming. Industrialized countries must recognize that their energy

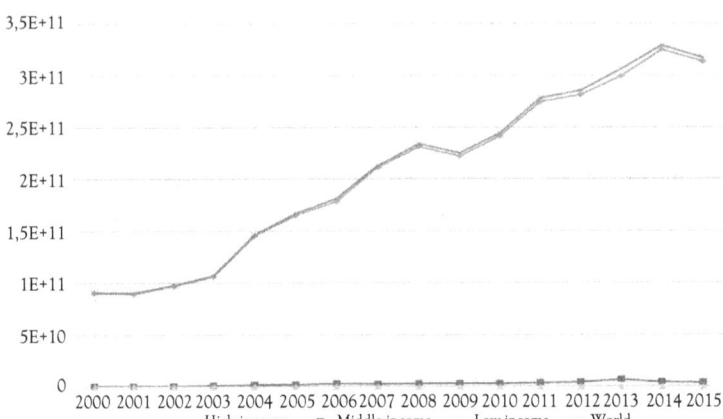

Figure 4.7 A key source of increasing the gap in growth and development between advanced and emerging/frontier economies

Source: Authors' calculations according to the World Bank database

consumption is polluting the biosphere and eating into scarce fossil fuel supplies. Recent improvements in energy efficiency and a shift toward less energy-intensive sectors have helped limit consumption, but the process must be accelerated to reduce per capita consumption and encourage a change to nonpolluting sources and technologies.

The prevention and reduction of air and water pollution will remain a critical task of resource conservation. Air and water quality come under pressure from such activities as fertilizer and pesticide use, urban sewage, fossil fuel burning, the use of certain chemicals, and various other industrial activities. Each of these is expected to increase the pollution load on the biosphere, particularly in developing countries. Cleaning up after the event is an expensive solution. Hence all countries need to anticipate and prevent these pollution problems by, for instance, enforcing emission standards that reflect long-term effects, promoting low-waste technologies, and anticipating the impact of new products, technologies, and wastes.

Figure 4.7 depicts one, if not a key, source of increasing the gap in growth and development between developed and developing countries, which adds to the unsustainability of the present form of capitalism. That source is creation and benefits from the creation of innovative technology which is almost entirely located in the developed part of the world.

Most of the developed technology is related, and income generated from it is the source of growth of the developed countries, countries of high income. In time this gap only widens. Technological lagging behind for the developing part of the world is a systemic problem for the present form of capitalism, which is evidence-based when it comes to the failure of the assumption that dissemination and creation of technology and then of productivity and innovation would spread from more to less developed countries.

Fostering Socioeconomic Developments

Socioeconomic development is inextricably linked to technology change, as technology, society, and institutions coevolve. Technology change can be a source of conflict, as well as a tool for social inclusion and greater cooperation. The UN takes an example of ICTs, which have allowed considerable advances in this respect, for instance, in health, education, transport, and communications, but they have led to security and privacy challenges.

A circular economy is one in which industrial systems are restorative and regenerative by intention and design. Creating a circular economy requires bringing together academia, the private sector, the public sector, and civil society. More sustainable production schemes and innovation in the private sector are needed. Countries need to explore their own desired paths of economic diversification based on the identification of promising technological trajectories and new industries. Empirical evidence shows that development is associated with the shift of labor from low- to high-productivity and high-wage activities. The changes in the composition of the economic system occurring during this process give rise to an increasing variety and complexity of economic activities. Increasing complexity is associated with higher levels of GDP and growth and reduction of inequality. That process is ultimately the result of innovation, and that is the reason why innovation is one of the central pillars of sustainable capitalism. Promising actions in all these strategies is the use of empirical data on production, exports, and innovation to identify specific technology trajectories to guide the transition toward sustainable capitalism.

Promising technological innovations and new industries can be identified, using patent databases, benchmarking early movers based on their comparative advantage, and/or by using the "product space" and measures of product complexity.

There are several techniques that will figure prominently in the course of sustainable capitalism, and a resource aid, including but not limited to:

1. **Bio-tech:** biotechnology, genomics, and proteomics; gene-editing technologies and custom-designed DNA sequence; genetically modified organisms (GMO); stem cells and human engineering; bio-catalysis; synthetic biology; sustainable agriculture tech

2. **Digital-tech**: big data technologies; Internet of Things; 5G mobile phones; 3-D printing and manufacturing; cloud computing platforms; open data technology; free and open-source; massive open online courses; micro-simulation; E-distribution; systems combining radio, mobile phone, satellite, GIS, and remote sensing data; data sharing technologies, including citizen science-enabling technologies; social media technologies; mobile apps to promote public engagement and behavioral change; prepaid system of electricity use and automatic meter reading; digital monitoring technologies; digital security technology

3. **Nano-tech**: Nano-imprint lithography; nanotechnology applications for decentralized water and wastewater treatment, desalination, and solar energy (nanomaterial solar cells); promising organic and inorganic nanomaterials, for example, graphene, carbon nanotubes, carbon Nano-dots and conducting polymers, perovskites, iron, cobalt, and nickel nanoparticles, and many others

4. **Neuro-tech**: Digital automation, including autonomous vehicles (driverless cars and drones), IBM Watson, e-discovery platforms for legal practice, personalization algorithms, artificial intelligence, speech recognition, robotics, smart technologies, cognitive computing; computational models of the human brain; mesoscience-powered virtual reality.

5. **Green-tech:** Circular economy: technologies for remanufacturing, technologies for product lifecycle extension such as reuse and refurbishment, and technologies for recycling; multifunctional infrastructures; technologies for integration of centralized systems and decentralized systems for services provided; CO_2 mitigation technol-

ogies; low energy and emission technology. Energy: modern cook-stoves with emissions comparable to those of LPG stove; deployment of off-grid electricity systems (and perhaps direct current); minigrids based on intermittent renewables with storage; advances in battery technology; heat pumps for space heating, heat and power storage and electric mobility (in interaction with off-grid electricity); smart grids; natural gas technologies; new ways of electrification; desalination (reverse osmosis); small- and medium-sized nuclear reactors; biofuel supply chains; solar photovoltaic, wind, and micro-hydro technologies; salinity gradient power technology; water-saving cooling technology; LED lamps; advanced metering. Transport: integrated public transport infrastructure, electric vehicles (e-car and e-bike), hydrogen-fueled vehicles, and supply infrastructures. Water: mobile water treatment technology, wastewater technology, advanced metering infrastructure. Buildings: sustainable building technology, passive housing. Agriculture: sustainable agriculture technology; innovations of bio-based products and processing, low input processing and storage technologies; horticulture techniques; irrigation technologies; bio-organometallics, which increase the efficiency of biomimetic analogs of nitrogenize. Other: marine Vibrioses, artificial photosynthesis

6. **Other technologies**: Assistive technologies for people with disabilities; alternative social technologies; fabrication laboratories; radical medical innovation; geoengineering technologies (e.g., for iron fertilization of oceans); new mining/extraction technologies (e.g., shale gas, in oceans, polar, glacier zones); deep-sea mining technologies

Threats are also present in potential form of unequal benefits, job losses, skills gaps, social impacts, poor people priced out; global value chain disruption; concerns about privacy, freedom, and development; data fraud, theft, cyber-attacks, human health (toxicity), environmental impact (nano-waste), deskilling, job polarization, widening technology gaps, military conflicts, and new inequalities.

At the global level, as depicted in Figure 4.8, GDP has not recuperated from the global setback caused by the financial crisis in 2008 and consequent 2009 recession or it is more accurate to state that developing

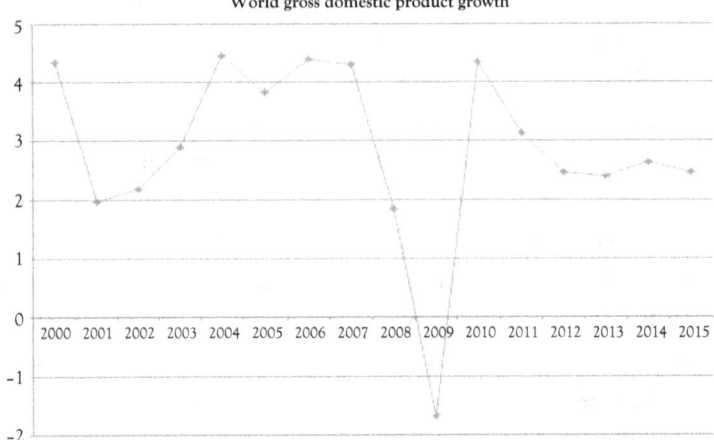

Figure 4.8 GDP has not recuperated from the global setback caused by financial crisis in 2008

Source: Authors' calculations according to World Bank database

part of the world has not recuperated from it but global implications of it are relatively present for the entire of the world GDP.

This means that development catching up would not be possible any time soon, and the gap between the rich and the poor would deepen again. Development that is sustainable has to address the problem of a large number of people who live in absolute poverty, that is, who are unable to satisfy even the most basic of their needs. Poverty reduces people's capacity to use resources in a sustainable manner; it intensifies pressure on the environment. Growth must be revived in developing countries because that is where the links between economic growth, the alleviation of poverty, and environmental conditions operate most directly. Yet developing countries are part of an interdependent world economy; their prospects also depend on the levels and patterns of growth in industrialized nations.

Capitalism is unsustainable if it increases vulnerability to crises. The vulnerability can be reduced by using technologies that lower production risks, by choosing institutional options that reduce market fluctuations, and by building up reserves, especially of food and foreign exchange. A development path that combines growth with reduced vulnerability is more sustainable than one that does not.

Sustainable capitalism requires views of human needs and well-being that incorporate such noneconomic variables as education and health enjoyed for their own sake, clean air and water, and the protection of natural beauty. Changing the quality of growth embedded in the notion of sustainable capitalism requires changing our approach to development efforts to take account of all of their effects. In some cases, sustainable capitalism will involve a rejection of activities that are financially attractive in the short run. Economic and social development can and should be mutually reinforcing. Money spent on education and health can raise human productivity. Economic developments can accelerate social development by providing opportunities for underprivileged groups or by spreading education more rapidly.

Infrastructure, in the broader sense, according to a UN document on global sustainability goals is defined as a means to fulfill a human need. It is composed of primary assets and objects that, in the aggregate, are deemed essential for the functioning of society and the economy. The scope of the infrastructure, as such comprises essential services such as water, sanitation, and energy, and connectivity infrastructure, including roads, transport systems, and information and communication technologies. Infrastructure affects inequality of outcomes and opportunities through three main channels:

1. Infrastructure providing essential services such as water, sanitation, and electricity may affect inequality depending on the quality, design, coverage, accessibility, and distribution of that infrastructure.
2. Infrastructure such as irrigation, electricity, ICT, and roads increases productivity and reduces trade costs, which affect the structural dynamics of the economy, including levels of income and distribution of jobs, and may have an effect on inequality.
3. Connectivity infrastructure, such as roads and ICT, affects the access of people to goods, services, and job opportunities, and therefore may affect inequality.

Environmental regulation must move beyond the usual menu of safety regulations, zoning laws, and pollution control enactments; environmental objectives must be built into taxation, prior approval procedures for investment and technology choice, foreign trade incentives, and all components of development policy. The integration of economic and ecological but also social factors into the law and decision-making systems within countries has to be matched at the international level. The growth in fuel and material use dictates that direct physical linkages between ecosystems of different countries will increase. Economic interactions through trade, finance, investment, and travel will also grow and heighten economic and ecological interdependence.

CHAPTER 5

Sustainable Capitalism in a Free-Market Economy: The U.S. Approach

Overview

The systems and institutions of free-market capitalism represented by the United States have proven their value over centuries by rising incomes and living standards not only for Americans but also for other nationals all over the world. No other economic system rivals capitalism for its productivity, dynamism, innovation, and wealth creation (Committee for Economic Development 2016). However, for the past decade or so, developed free-market economies, including the United States, have been exposing the international business world and global investors to numerous risks, starting from the U.S. economy trembling during the financial crisis in 2008. To respond to the challenges, Gore and Blood (2011) proposed to abandon short-term economic thinking for "sustainable capitalism" and claimed:

Before the crisis and since, we and others have called for a more responsible form of capitalism, what we call sustainable capitalism: a framework that seeks to maximize long-term economic value by reforming markets to address real needs while integrating environmental, social and governance (ESG) metrics throughout the decision-making process.

Such sustainable capitalism applies to the entire investment value chain—from entrepreneurial ventures to large public companies, seed-capital providers to institutional investors, employees to CEOs, activists to policy makers. It transcends borders, industries, asset classes, and stakeholders.[1]

But it was just a start.

---

[1] https://www.algore.com/news/a-manifesto-for-sustainable-capitalism

A Manifesto for Sustainable Capitalism

Former Vice-President Al Gore and former Goldman Sachs banker David Blood not only issued a white paper together in 2012 to systematically introduce the concept of "Sustainable Capitalism" but also cofounded a long-term sustainable investment firm named Generation Investment Management LLP (GIM) in 2004. GIM pioneered a new type of investing, emphasizing long-term financial returns through sustainable projects with about $12 billion under its management in 2016 (Zhuo 2016).

Gore and Blood (2011) recommend five critical actions for immediate adoption by the business community under sustainable capitalism:

1. Identify and incorporate risk from "stranded assets." They define "stranded assets" as those whose value would dramatically change, either positively or negatively, when significant externalities, such as attributing a reasonable price to carbon or water, are taken into account. Stranded assets are the ones with the potential to trigger substantial reductions in the long-term value of not just particular firms but entire industries.

2. Mandate integrated reporting. Integrated reporting would enable firms and investors to make better resource allocation decisions by seeing how ESG performance contributes to sustainable, long-term value creation. Access to more data for equity investors has not necessarily translated into more comprehensive insight into firms. Integrated reporting offers a solution to such a problem by encouraging firms to combine both their financial results and ESG performance into one report covering only the most salient or material metrics. While voluntary integrated reporting is becoming more popular, to ensure swift and broad adoption, it must be mandated by appropriate policy makers such as stock exchanges and securities regulators.

3. End the default practice of issuing quarterly earnings guidance. Currently, the quarterly filings, mandated by the SEC for public firms listed in the U.S. stock markets, often incentivize executives to manage for the short term. It also encourages some investors to overreact to the significance of these short-term measures at the expense of longer-term, more profound measures of sustainable value creation.

By ending this practice, firms will issue guidance only as they deem appropriate and would encourage a longer-term view of the business.

4. Align compensation structures with long-term sustainable performance. To echo the adjustment of financial reporting and earnings guidance, most present compensation schemes need to be reviewed and modified as well. The existing ones emphasize short-term actions and fail to hold corporate executives and asset managers accountable for the ramifications of their decisions over the long term. Proposed financial rewards should be paid out over the period during which the results are realized. Compensation should be associated with fundamental drivers of long-term value, employing rolling multiyear milestones for performance evaluation.

5. Incentivize long-term investing with loyalty-driven securities. This initiative is designed to change the dominance of short-termism in the market, which fosters general market volatility and undermines the efforts of firm executives seeking long-term sustainable value creation.

Environmental	Social	Governance
• Air quality output	• Access and a affordability of	• Accounting and audit process
• Bidiversity impacts	product or service	• Board composition
• Carbon footprint	• Consumer rights	• Business ethics
• Climate change resiliency	• Corporate philanthropy	• Compliance
• Energy consumption	• Customer relations	• Executive remuneration
• Environmental policy	• Data security and customer	• Lobbying and political
• Fresh water use	privacy	contributions
• Ground water depletion	• Diversity issues	• Ownership structure
• Impacts on the cryosphere	• Employee engagement	• Reporting and disclosure
• Impacts on the food supply	• Fair disclosure and labelling	• Shareholder rights
• Land use	• Health and safety of	• Succession planning
• Bidiversity impacts	communities	• Transparency
• Natural resource management	• Human capital management	• Voting procedures
• Ocean productivity and	• Human rights	
acidification	• Labour relations	*Additional considerations for funds...*
• Regulatory & legal risks	• Product quality and safety	• Advisory committee powers
• Supply chain management	• Responsible R&D	and composition
• Vulnerability to extreme	• Stakeholder and community	• Client alignment & fee
weather	relations	structure
• Waste & hazardous materials	• Supply chain management	• Fund governance
management		

Figure 5.1 Key ESG factors defined[2]

Source: Analysis by the Generation Foundation

---

[2] The Generation Foundation. 2015. *Allocating Capital for Long-Term Returns.*

Sustainable capitalism has been a hot topic since its introduction and is referred by other names at times, such as Long-Term Capitalism, Inclusive Capitalism, Inclusive Prosperity, and Shared Value. It is an economic system within which business and capital seek to maximize long-term value creation and accounting for all material ESG metrics. It considers all costs and benefits, regardless of whether they are currently attributed to an economic "price tag" by society. Figure 5.1 provides the key components of each ESG factor defined. Sustainable capitalism aims to tackle real issues in all economic, business, financial, and policy decisions, which transcend borders, sectors, asset classes, forms of ownership, and stakeholders. In reality, it exists at the intersection of business, science, politics, and market forces (The Generation Foundation 2015).

Current Challenges

(Free-) market capitalism has proven to be a remarkable engine of wealth creation, but if it continues to function in the next 25 years as it has in the past 25, we are in for a violent ride or, worse, a serious breakdown in the system itself. (Bower, Leonard, and Paine 2011)

In 2008, slightly before Gore and Blood issued their sustainable capitalism white paper, to prepare for Harvard Business School's 100th anniversary Global Business Summit focusing on the future of market capitalism, a small group of business and government leaders around the world participated in a survey regarding what issues should inform the school's agenda for the new century. The survey results showed that a primary concern for virtually all of the participants was the long-term sustainability of global market capitalism. Several critical challenges identified in the survey were the following:

- Environmental degradation. Industrial growth is accompanied by climate change, which affects the availability of air quality, water, sea levels, and the health of crops. The consequences could be observed in migration, the disruption of production and trade, and political instability.

- The fragility of the financial system. Trillions of dollars move at high velocities around the world every day, but with little transparency. These unmanaged and unregulated flows can compound risk with devastating consequences such as the financial crisis of 2008.
- Inequality and populism. The growing income and wealth disparities within countries and across regions are increasing, which disproves the concept that economic growth benefits all. Inequality could lead to harmful government interventions, including confiscation of property and overregulation of market transactions.
- The rise of state capitalism. Developing countries have adopted variations of mercantilist policies, especially state capitalism, to accelerate economic growth for centuries. After the recent financial crisis, major emerging economies led by China and Russia who play their own rules focusing on state control demonstrate the potential to disrupt free-market capitalism, which is practiced in the developed world.
- The inadequacy of institutions. International cooperation often consists of ad hoc agreements to address climate change, trade, and migration challenges. It is the systemic character of the current challenges that makes them complex and difficult to address. The existing disruptive forces interact in negative ways so that problems in one area stimulate new ones in others. Neither governments nor international institutions are set up and ready to deal with systemic failure (Bower et al. 2011).

Environmental Breakdown and Its Causes

To echo Bower et al.'s (2011) findings, according to the "Sustainability Trends Report—2019," recently issued by GIM, the United States, together with other countries in the world, is facing enormous challenges entering an age of environmental breakdown. The social and economic fabric is fraying measured by ESG metrics (Generation Investment Management 2019).

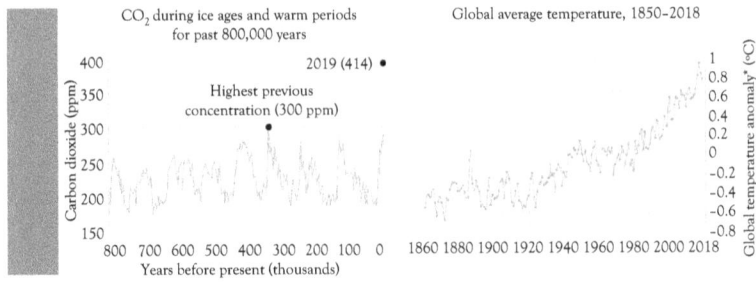

* Relative to 1951-1980 average

Figure 5.2 Global CO$_2$ emissions and average global temperatures continue to rise[3]

Source: NOAA; Berkeley Earth; Mauna Loa Observatory, Hawaii

The world fails to meet many of the 2030 Sustainable Development Goals with potentially disastrous outcomes. In 2019, CO$_2$ concentration levels are at 414 parts per million (ppm), far beyond the previous highs in history. Global greenhouse gas (CO$_2$) emissions and average global temperatures continue to rise (Figure 5.2), which created an environmental crisis with clearly negative economic and social impacts. The scale of the needed transformation is revolutionary. It means transitioning away from an incumbent energy system, which has relied on fossil fuels for more than 150 years, is inevitable and would lead to a dramatic change in global environmental policies.

The environmental crisis has substantial economic and social consequences. Figure 5.3 shows global insured losses from catastrophes in 2017 at more than $140 billion, and in 2018 at $79 billion and a likely rise in climate refugees since 2010.

One major cause of the environment breakdown is the source of energy. According to Lawrence Livermore National Laboratory's most recently published data (Table 5.1), U.S. energy use totaled 101.2 quads in 2018. A quad is equal to 1 quadrillion BTUs, which is approximately equivalent to 185 million barrels of crude oil, 8 billion gallons of gasoline, or 1 trillion cubic feet of natural gas. Fossil fuels, which directly caused

---

[3] Sustainability Trends Report - 2019, by Generation Investment Management LLP. https://generationim.com/sustainability-trends/sustainability-trends-2019/

CO_2 emissions and climate change, accounted for over 80 percent in the U.S. energy consumption mix from 2014 to 2018.

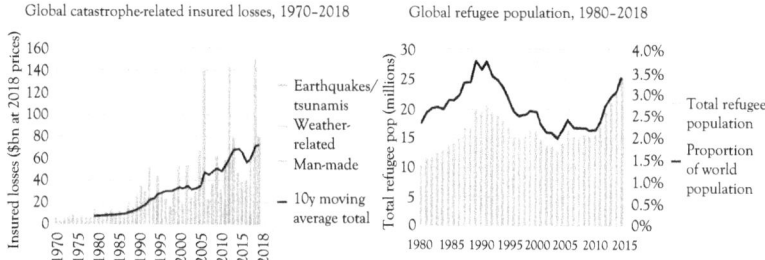

Global catastrophe-related insured losses, 1970-2018   Global refugee population, 1980-2018

* According to the European Parliament, Climate refugees are "migrants who move due to natural disasters and climate change"

Figure 5.3 *Global insured losses from catastrophes keep growing and a probable increase of climate refugees after the recent financial crisis[4]*

Source: Swiss Re, UNCHR

In addition to heavy reliance on fossil fuels with severe environmental and social impacts, one noticeable fact indicated in Figure 5.4 is that rejected energy, which represents the energy that actually gets wasted due to various inefficiencies, consumed 68 percent of all power generated in 2018 (Lawrence Livermore National Laboratory 2018).

Table 5.1 *U.S. energy consumption and % fossil fuels in the mix from 2014 to 2018. Energy use measured in quads (1 quadrillion BTUs)[5]*

Year	U.S. energy consumption	% of fossil fuels in mix
2018	101.2 quads	80.2%
2017	97.7 quads	80.0%
2016	97.3 quads	80.8%
2015	97.2 quads	81.6%
2014	98.3 quads	81.6%

[4] Sustainability Trends Report - 2019, by Generation Investment Management LLP. https://generationim.com/sustainability-trends/sustainability-trends-2019/
[5] Data from Lawrence Livermore National Laboratory

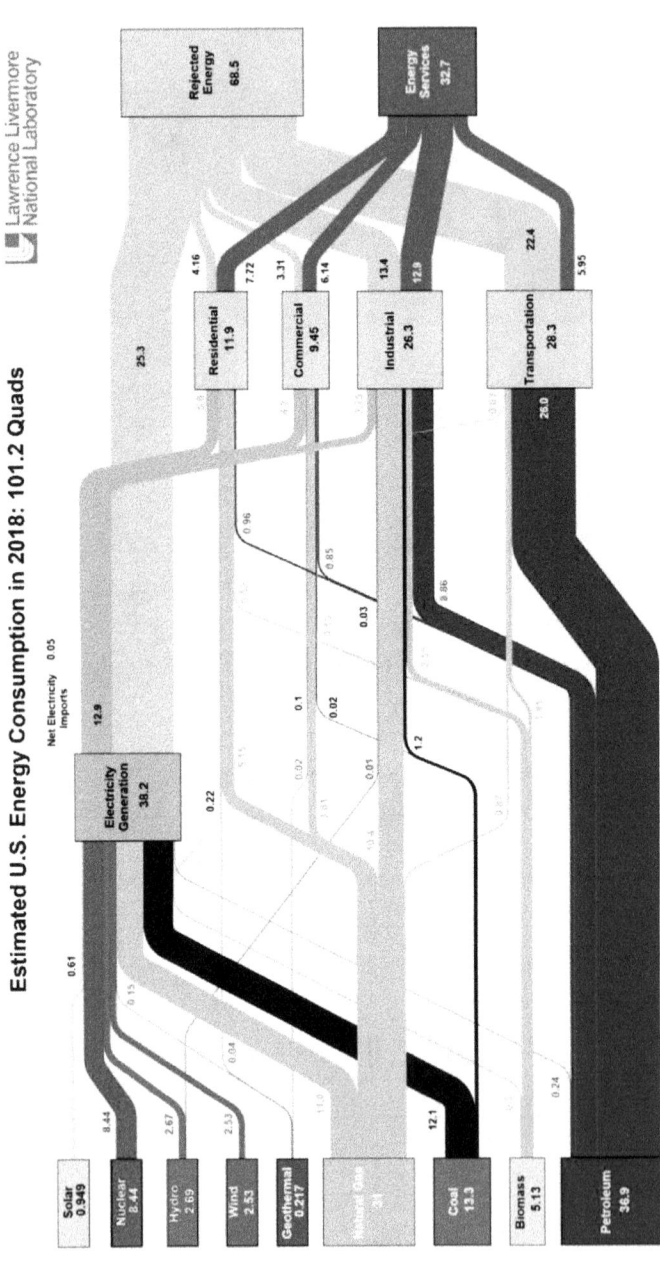

Figure 5.4 All U.S. energy use in one Sankey diagram, including the original energy source (i.e., nuclear, oil, wind) as well as the ultimate end use (i.e., residential, commercial) for the energy that was generated. Data from Lawrence Livermore National Laboratory

It is evident that the current model of energy consumption and sources is not sustainable. Replacing the burning of fossil fuels with clean energy becomes a crucial step in supporting long-term economic growth, eliminating pollution, and protecting public health.

"Stranded Assets" and Their Determination

The examination of U.S. energy consumption and sources leads to a new question "How to balance economic needs and growth while integrating ESG metrics throughout the decision-making process?"

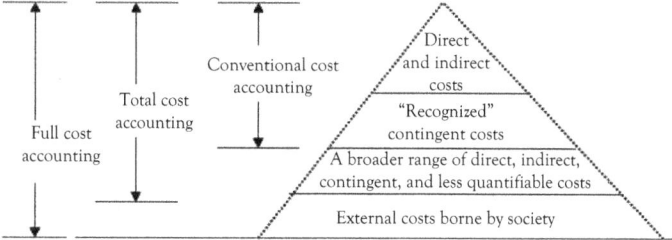

Figure 5.5 Relationships between forms of accounting and financial reporting[6]

One solution proposed by Gore and Blood (2011) is to identify and incorporate risk from stranded assets. They define "stranded assets" as those whose value would dramatically change, either positively or negatively, when significant externalities are taken into account. To address energy consumption and CO_2 emissions caused by fossil fuels, the market should attribute a reasonable price to carbon. As shown in Figure 5.5, the existing financial reporting systems (both U.S. Generally accepted accounting principles (GAAP) and International Financial Reporting Standards (IFRS)) only report direct, indirect, and "recognized" contingent costs without quantifying and reflecting externalities, such as environmental costs. Such omissions lead to "stranded assets," which have the potential to trigger significant reductions in the long-term value of not just particular firms but entire industries. The world's top body on accounting, the International Federation of Accountants (IFAC), also said that financial reporting is critical, but it's not sufficient.

---

[6] Government of Canada. 2007. *Pollution Prevention Planning Handbook.*

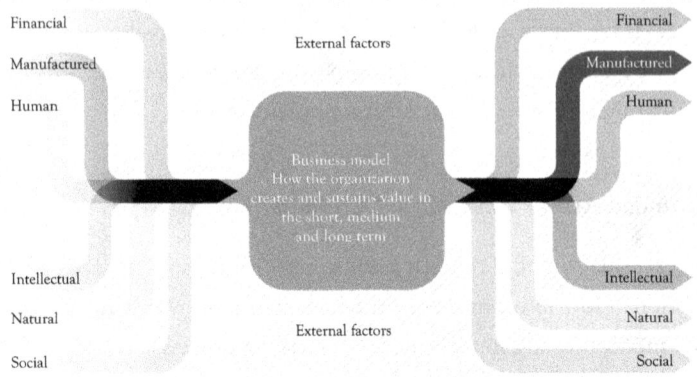

Figure 5.6 Integrated reporting framework to visualize the business model in which an organization uses different capitals (financial, manufactured, human, intellectual, natural, and social)[7]

It becomes an important task to change the mindset and practice of current financial reporting systems to include ESG metrics and to determine the true value of "stranded assets" for long-term decisions. Figure 5.6 shows the framework of integrated reporting, which covers not only financial, manufactured, human, and intellectual capital, but also two relatively new capitals need to be considered:

1. Natural capital, which is an input to the production of goods or the provision of services. A firm's activities also impact, positively or negatively, on natural capital including:

   • Water, land, minerals, and forests; and
   • Biodiversity and ecosystem health.

2. Social capital, which is the institutions and relationships established within and between each community, group of stakeholders, and other networks to enhance individual and collective well-being (Integrated Reporting 2011).

---

[7] Integrated Reporting. 2011. *Towards Integrated Reporting-Communicating Value in the 21st Century.*

Possible Solutions and Development

We (the United States) are once again facing one of those rare turning points in history when dangerous challenges and limitless opportunities cry out for clear, long-term thinking. The disruptive threats now facing the planet are extraordinary: climate change, water scarcity, poverty, disease, growing income inequality, urbanization, massive economic volatility, and more. (Gore and Blood 2011)

Duly acknowledging the fundamental and historical merits of U.S. free-market capitalism, its future success will depend upon the willingness to maintain the fundamental principles of free-market capitalism. An effective free-market economic system needs to properly allocate resources of financial, manufactured, human, intellectual, natural, and social, which includes relationship capital suggested by King (2016). Such allocation should be both accurate (resources get to their best uses) and efficient (the allocation should be accomplished at the lowest possible cost). If the economic system achieves that fundamental objective, then it would be expected to result in the robust formation of new and innovative businesses, improvement of productivity and living standards and sustainable and healthy economic growth to adequately address the aforementioned key challenges and issues (Committee for Economic Development 2016).

Integrated Thinking and Reporting

It is critical to have accurate and integrated information to support resource allocation decisions as an essential part of free-market capitalism.

Research conducted by Graham, Harvey, and Rajgopal (2005) and Dichev, Graham, Harvey, and Rajgopal (2013) offer perspectives from the practitioners who prepare financial reports (CFOs) serving as the vital information source for external decision makers. Earnings indicated by earnings per share (EPS) remain as the key metric on top of CFOs' priority list; 74 percent of CFOs consider analyst consensus estimate or expectations as the earnings benchmark (Graham et al. 2005). Meeting or beating analyst forecast is critical to them to build credibility with the capital market, maintain or increase the firm's stock price, and enhance the external reputation of management. Moreover, Dichev et al. (2013) find that managers rank "To influence stock price" as the most critical motivation to manipulate earnings (93% of survey respondents) since they (95%) believe that earnings are used by investors in valuing the company. In reality, 99 percent of CFOs believe that at least some firms manage earnings, and roughly 20 percent of the firms manipulated earnings in any given period in which 10 percent of the earnings number was managed (Lin, Xia, and Bardhan 2019).

The survey results provide evidence to demonstrate that the current pattern of communication between firms and stakeholders perpetuates and reinforces short-termism in the capital market. Furthermore, there is insufficient sustainability disclosure in terms of both the quality of the content and the volume of reporting, which make the decision-making process imperceptive and inefficient.

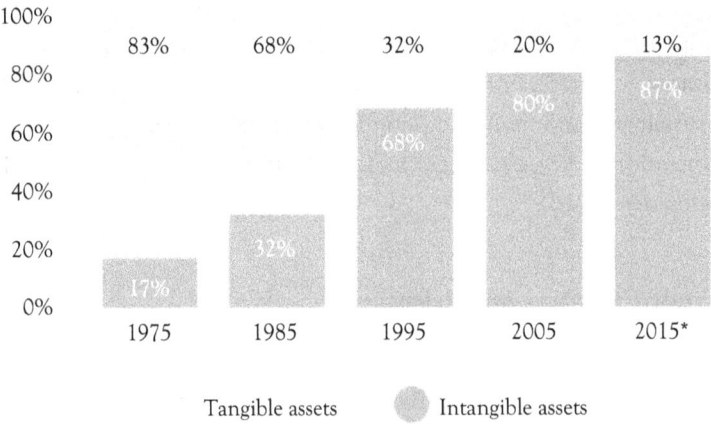

Figure 5.7 *Components of the S&P 500 market value evolved from 1975 to 2015*[8]

Source: Ocean Tomo, LLC

---

[8] Stathis, K.L. 2015. *Ocean Tomo Releases 2015 Annual Study of Intangible Asset Market Value.*

Another aspect related to accurate reporting, which is especially important in a modern market with shifting macroeconomic values, wherein an average of 87 percent of the market value of companies in 2015 lied in intangible assets (Figure 5.7). However, accounting practices and processes remain outdated, with a biased focus on the short term (Stathis 2015).

The right approach to provide complete and accurate information is using integrated thinking from the concept of the total value, which looks at the firm's impact on three critical aspects: the economy, society, and the environment. Integrated thinking covers six capitals required in business model in total value creation: financial, manufactured, human, intellectual, natural, and social capital, in short, medium, and long terms. Integrated thinking is transparent, concise, and materialistic and is supported by new information technologies. It is understanding, knowing, and then planning how the firm creates value and sustainably generates profit, knowing the demand for products is growing, and yet there are less natural assets (King 2016).

The development of integrated thinking results in integrated reporting, which is designed to enhance and consolidate existing reporting practices that provide the information needed to assess organizational value and make sound investment decisions. Integrated reporting

> brings together material information about an organization's strategy, governance, performance, and prospects in a way that reflects the commercial, social, and environmental context within which it operates. It provides a clear and concise representation of how an organization demonstrates stewardship and how it creates and sustains value. An Integrated Report should be an organization's primary reporting vehicle. (Integrated Reporting 2011)

Integrated reporting offers a broader explanation of performance than traditional financial reporting. Integrated Reporting (2011) points out that integrated reporting makes visible a firm's use of and dependence on different resources and relationships or "capitals" (financial, manufactured, human, intellectual, natural, and social) and the firm's access to and impact on them. Reporting this information is extremely important and meaningful to:

- Overall assessment of the long-term viability of the firm's business model and strategy;
- Meeting the information needs of investors and other stakeholders; and
- Ultimately, the effective allocation of scarce resources.

In the real business world, the first stakeholder report was issued by Ben and Jerry (now owned by Unilever) in Vermont in 1995. In 1998, Bob Massie and Allen White, partnering with the United Nations and major U.S. foundations, cofounded the Global Reporting Initiative (GRI). Intel, in March 2010, made sustainability a fiduciary duty by amending its corporate charter to include mandatory reporting on "corporate responsibility and sustainability performance." The Johannesburg Stock Exchange in South Africa set an exemplary precedent in 2011 to require all listed companies to either produce an integrated report or explain why they were not doing so. According to the most recent 2017 database, 10,613 organizations have produced 40,155 reports, of which 26,675 are GRI reports.

The Generation Foundation contributes to the integrated reporting initiative by providing seed funding to the Sustainability Accounting Standards Board (SASB) and contributing to industry knowledge through various working groups and consultations. In 2012, SASB, a not-for-profit organization, was founded in California. Its mission is to establish a much clearer understanding of material sustainability risks and opportunities facing firms and to create crucial industry-based performance indicators suitable for disclosure in standard filings with the U.S. Securities and Exchange Commission (SEC). To date, SASB has issued reviews on 7 of its 10 specified sectors and has launched both a corporate pilot program and a software provider partnership program to help companies integrate SASB standards into their disclosure processes. Meanwhile, to establish a framework for integrated reporting, the International Integrated Reporting Council (IIRC), which is composed of an international cross-section of leaders from the corporate, investment, accounting, securities, regulatory, academic, civil society, and standard-setting sectors, solicited commitments from 140 businesses and 26 investors worldwide for its pilot program which was concluded in September 2014 (The Generation Foundation 2015).

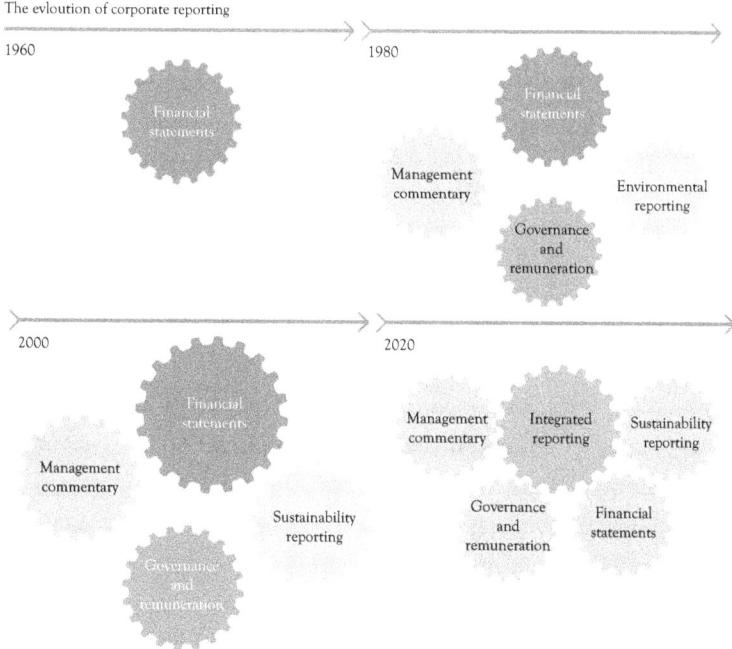

Figure 5.8 The evolution from traditional financial reporting to integrated reporting with a focus on sustainability[9]

The evolution and mandating of integrated reporting are just a starting point, as reporting standards around ESG information and its link to financial metrics will need to be refined continuously (Figure 5.8).

The Association of Certified Chartered Accountants (ACCA), one of the most influential organizations of public accountants, believes

> Over the past few decades, sustainability issues have slowly become mainstream, and there is a shift from the creation of share value to a generation of shared value. Through shared value creation, a company links its operations to generating long-term value both for its business and for society as a whole and defines its success in terms of internal financial returns and external social and economic results. Ultimately, creating shared value acknowl-

---

[9] Integrated Reporting. 2011. *Towards Integrated Reporting-Communicating Value in the 21st Century.*

edges both the work that corporations need to do to reduce negative impacts on society as well as, and more fundamentally, how they can be part of progress on global challenges, such as climate change and the enforcement of human rights. Following this shift, there is a new trend of corporate reporting: the integration of financial and nonfinancial concerns into one accounting tool, known as integrated reporting. (ACCA & IMA 2016)

For the future direction, Generation Investment Management (2012)

propose(s) integrated reporting be mandated for publicly listed companies by the appropriate regulatory agencies, and we encourage voluntary action by these companies in the short term to provide integrated reports until such regulation comes to pass. We also encourage investors to ask for integrated reports from their portfolio companies, including private equity investors, and that they incorporate this information in their investment decisions. Additionally, we support the growing commitment by privately held companies to produce integrated reports.

Accelerate Sustainable Energy Innovation

With integrated thinking and reporting to fully cover ESG metrics and their link to financial results, it makes ESG metrics a crucial consideration in any long-term decisions related to sustainability. Replacing the burning of fossil fuels in transportation, industrial, and residential and commercial buildings with clean electricity is a critical step to maintain sustainable growth and preventing catastrophic climate change.

Table 5.2 summarizes the transformation in related industries with low carbon and resource-efficient solutions backed by innovative technologies. The most substantial percentage increases in the energy consumption mix have come from solar, which increased by 122 percent and wind sources which increased by 46 percent from 2014 to 2018 (Table 5.3). However, solar and wind only account for 0.94 and 2.5 percent, respectively, in the energy consumption mix in 2018, which indicates their limited shares but with tremendous growth potential.

Table 5.2 The innovative transformation of various industries as the United States decarbonizes

Industry	Low carbon and resource efficient innovation			
Energy	Solar	Wind	Geothermal	Storage
Buildings	Insulating Materials	Lighting	Metering	Appliances
Transport	Engines	Electric Vehicles	Fleet logistics	Biofuels
Water	Irrigation	Desalination	Wastewater	Distribution
Materials	Biochemical	Biodegradable	Nanomaterials	Plastics
Recycling	Reverse logistics	Meterial sorting	Sharing goods	Waste to energy
Environmental Intelligence	Big Data	Data centre efficiency	Remote sensing	Local Digital platforms
Agriculture	Meat replacement	Forestry management	Urban farming	Precision agriculture

Source: Analysis by The Generation Fundation

Table 5.3 U.S. energy consumption sources from solar and wind from 2014 to 2018. Energy use measured in quads (1 quadrillion BTUs)[10]

Source	2014	2015	2016	2017	2018	Change ('14-'18)
Solar	0.427	0.426	0.587	0.775	0.949	+122%
Wind	1.73	1.78	2.11	2.35	2.53	+46%

As Figure 5.9 shows, among 50 states, some (especially the ones in the northeast and northwest) are doing impressively well to generate electricity by no fossil fuel to address the environmental challenges. Vermont leads the way with a remarkable 99.6 percent mix for electricity generated by hydro. New Hampshire takes another path to reach 77 percent with its heavy usage of nuclear (Table 5.4), including the state's Seabrook nuclear plant (1,244 MW), which is the largest individual electrical generating unit on the New England power grid. Four out of the top five states achieving a high percentage of green energy mainly rely on hydro as their energy sources (Lawrence Livermore National Laboratory 2018).

---

[10] Data from Lawrence Livermore National Laboratory.

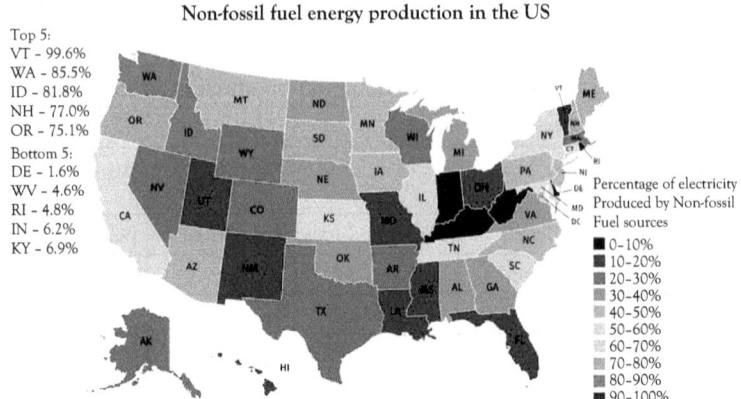

Figure 5.9 Percentage of electricity produced by no fossil fuel sources by state[11]

Regarding rejected energy, Figure 5.4 indicates that 68 percent of all power generated is not harnessed for any productive use, in which 22.4 percent is caused by transportation since most vehicle gasoline engines are only about 20 to 40 percent efficient. This makes the electric vehicle an appealing solution as the electric engine is 85 to 90 percent efficient plus its consumption of environmentally friendly clean energy. The total number of electric vehicles sold in the United States went beyond 1.2 million from December 2010 to May 2019. Tesla clearly took the lead, with 409,465 cars sold or 33 percent market share during that period (Figure 5.10).

Table 5.4 The top five states producing electricity with green energy[12]

Rank State	State	% of green energy	Top energy source
#1	Vermont	99.60%	Hydro
#2	Washington	85.50%	Hydro
#3	Idaho	81.80%	Hydro
#4	New Hampshire	77.00%	Nuclear
#5	Oregon	75.10%	Hydro

---

[11] Data from The U.S. Energy Information Administration (EIA). https://eia.gov/electricity/data/browser/

[12] Data from Lawrence Livermore National Laboratory.

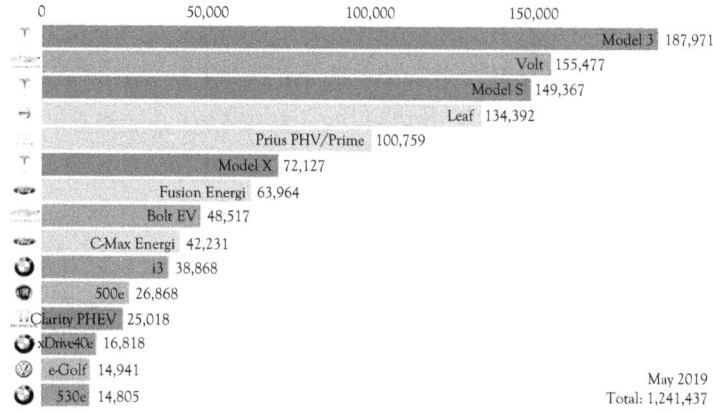

Figure 5.10 Number of electric vehicles sold in the United States from December 210 to May 2019[13]

The business community also plays an active role in exploring a clean energy solution. RE100 is a global corporate leadership initiative bringing together influential businesses committed to 100 percent renewable electricity. Close to 200 RE100 companies have committed to going 100 percent renewable (Generation Investment Management, 2019). Figure 5.11 shows that U.S. firms have been dominant players in the world market in using clean power in their supply chains since 2013.

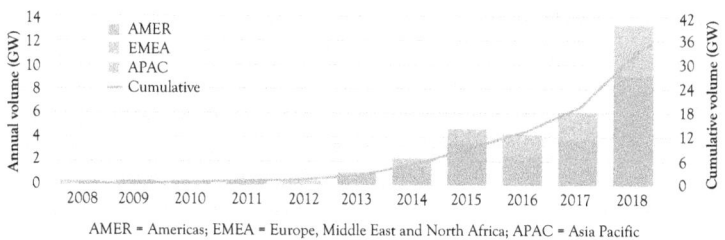

Figure 5.11 Corporate purchases of clean power, 2008–2018[14]

---

[13] Data from InsideEVs. https://insideevs.com/

[14] Data from Bloomberg New Energy Finance.

The U.S. government, firms, and research institutions are working together to accelerate sustainable energy innovation to become more environmentally friendly and more efficiently allocate natural resources to support the sustainable growth of the country's free-market economy.

Corporate Green Investment and Capital Market

From electricity produced by green energy sources to electric vehicles to reduce rejected energy and increase energy efficiency, the rapid growth of sustainable energy innovation comes at a price. The United Nations Conference on Trade and Development (UNCTAD) estimates that the cost of delivering the United Nations Sustainable Development Goals (SDGs), a roadmap to a more sustainable future for the world which was established in September 2015, could be between $5 and $7 trillion per year, and there is about $2.5 trillion funding gap every year in developing countries. The related green investment needs to be mobilized jointly and urgently from the public, private, and multilateral sources.

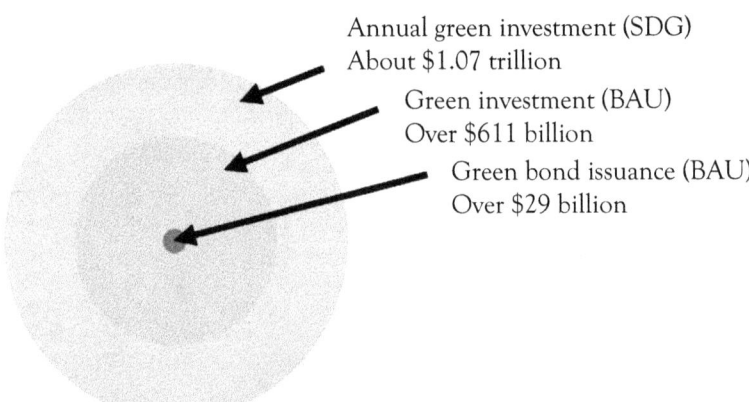

Annual green investment (SDG)
About $1.07 trillion

Green investment (BAU)
Over $611 billion

Green bond issuance (BAU)
Over $29 billion

Figure 5.12 Green investments and green bond issuance by large firms: goals versus reality[15]

(SDG): The UN SDG scenario. (BAU): the business as usual scenario.

The corporate world, especially the large firms, plays a vital role in effective and efficient resource allocation in free-market capitalism.

---

[15] Data from Corporate Knights and Climate Bond Initiative. March 2019.

largest firms, representing all publicly traded companies with $1 billion+ in revenues. These companies had an estimated $117 trillion in assets under management and loan books held via publicly traded financial corporations. They also made capital and R&D expenditures of $3.6 trillion in 2017. Corporate Knights' research methodology measures the green investment funding gap of large firms between two scenarios:

1. The UN SDG (SDG) scenario estimates green investment levels required to close the SDG funding gap, based on estimates by the Global Infrastructure Hub and Corporate Knights/Climate Bonds Initiative.
2. The business as usual (BAU) scenario examines current levels of corporate green investment via capital expenditure and R&D channels.

Figure 5.12 demonstrates the funding gap of $459 billion in 2017 between the SDG scenario of $1.07 trillion and the BAU scenario of $611 billion. The actual corporate green investment needs to be increased by 75 percent to meet UN SDG. Furthermore, there was only $29 billion or less than five percent of the existing $611 billion corporate green investments funded by the corporate green bond. The results indicate urgent needs and significant opportunities for increasing corporate green investment and corporate green bonds issuance (Corporate Knights 2019).

To examine corporate green investment at a more detailed level, Corporate Knights issued its "2019 Global 100 report" to rank the most sustainable corporations in the world. Again, Corporate Knights focused on publicly traded companies with $1 billion+ in revenues, which are screened for various factors such as sufficient sustainability reporting. The resulting corporations are scored on an industry-specific mix of performance metrics in the following areas:

• Resource management
• Employee management
• Financial management
• Clean revenue
• Supplier performance

Table 5.5 Three countries with the world's most sustainable companies[16]

Country	Number of companies on the global 100
United States	22
France	11
Japan	8

As the leader of free-market capitalism, the United States tops the list with 22 of the Global 100 companies—far more than any other country (Table 5.5). However, the largest developing nations of China and India notably have no representation on the list.

A closer look at 2019 Global 100 ranking of the world's most sustainable companies captures some common characteristics:

- Strong sustainability. Analysis by Corporate Knights with Thomson Reuters Datastream shows that the Global 100 companies have an average age of 87 years, while the average age of companies in the MSCI All Country World Index (ACWI) is 63 years.
- High profitability. From its inception in February 2005 to the end of 2018, the Global 100 delivered a net return on investment of 127.35 percent, compared to 118.27 percent for the MSCI ACWI. As contributive members of society, the Global 100 pay more taxes on average of 18 percent of EBITDA compared to 16 percent of the MSCI ACWI.
- More environmental friendly. The Global 100 firms have double the carbon productivity (weighted average of $238k in revenue per ton of CO_2 emissions versus $157k for the MSCI ACWI) and derive 26 percent of their revenues from green goods and services versus 9 percent for the MSCI ACWI.

---

[16] Data from Corporate Knights 2019 Global 100 report.

- Better corporate governance. The Global 100 firms have a lower CEO-to-average-worker pay ratio (76:1) than the MSCI ACWI (140:1), which is a mandatory disclosure set by SEC to address the growing concern about income inequality. The Global 100 have a tighter link between sustainability measures and executive pay (58 percent have a link vs. 19 percent for the MSCI ACWI). They also have more females on their boards (average 27 percent vs. 19 percent for the MSCI ACWI).

In summary, the comparison between the Global 100 firms and MSCI ACWI companies suggests that performing well on sustainability issues not only generates superior financial performance but also brings better corporate governance and transparency, which makes them a better choice to the investors (Scott 2019).

On the other hand, investors are looking for firms with less risk exposure in corporate governance, environmental factors, and human rights (Figure 5.13). Investors believe that using ESG criteria vastly decreases unnecessary risks. The additional considerations serving as potential risk filters are corporate governance, working practices, environmental hazards, human rights, and social impact.

Due to information asymmetry, for investors as external stakeholders, sustainability is a primary but reliable tool to identify well-run firms with a long-term view and sustainable growth potential. Oppositely, risks related to sustainability, if not adequately addressed, can negatively affect the total valuation of the company and investment decisions. According to a recent Ernst & Young (EY) study, 87 percent of investors will reconsider or change their minds, if they know a company that they're investing has risk or history of poor environmental performance (Figure 5.13). EY study, in turn, proves that firms with the Global 100 characteristics are more welcome in the capital market.

Currently, $23 trillion out of the $85 trillion of assets under management globally incorporate nonfinancial information such as ESG data in their investment criteria, and that figure is growing by 25 percent every year (Tavares 2018).

To better attract investment to firms with sustainability, another issue needing to be addressed is short-termism.

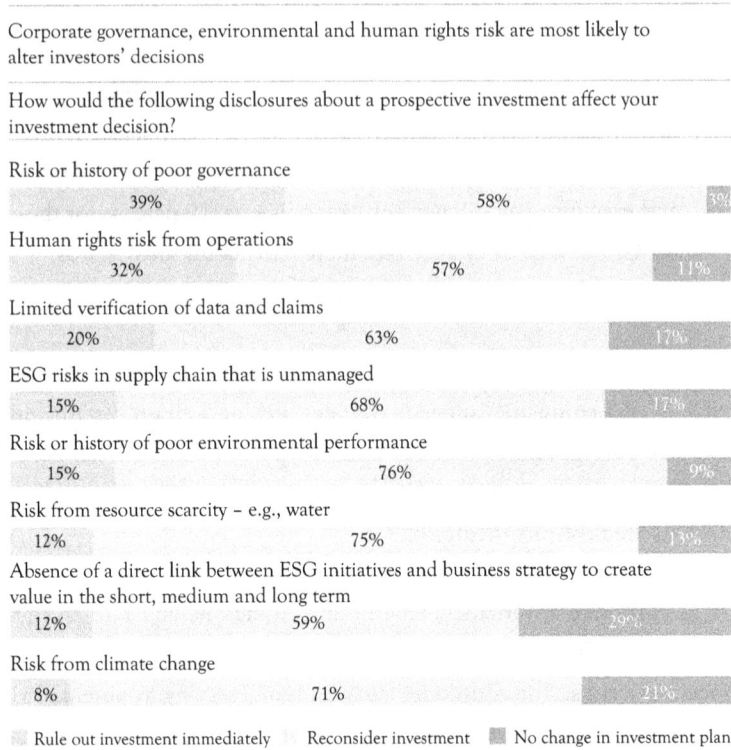

Corporate governance, environmental and human rights risk are most likely to alter investors' decisions

How would the following disclosures about a prospective investment affect your investment decision?

Risk or history of poor governance

39%   58%   3%

Human rights risk from operations

32%   57%   11%

Limited verification of data and claims

20%   63%   17%

ESG risks in supply chain that is unmanaged

15%   68%   17%

Risk or history of poor environmental performance

15%   76%   9%

Risk from resource scarcity – e.g., water

12%   75%   13%

Absence of a direct link between ESG initiatives and business strategy to create value in the short, medium and long term

12%   59%   29%

Risk from climate change

8%   71%   21%

Rule out investment immediately   Reconsider investment   No change in investment plan

Figure 5.13 Key risks which would impact investors' decisions
Source: EY

Today, the average mutual fund in the U.S. turns over its entire portfolio every seven months; 20 years ago, it was every seven years. Something has fundamentally changed, and the problem with that is it means we're not making good investing decisions... and not delivering proper and efficient wealth creation

While we accept that investors may have to sell stock for reasons that are beyond their control (e.g., a change in actuarial models that requires a portfolio reallocation) and that carefully balancing time-horizons with appropriate levels of liquidity is essential, the dominance of short-termism in the market—facilitated by algorithmic trading—is correlated with stock price volatility. This, in turn, fosters general market instability as opposed to useful liquidity and undermines the efforts of executives who are trying to manage for long-term value creation (Generation Investment Management 2012).

This growing trend toward short-termism, together with the increasing volatility it creates in the markets, sequentially, can hurt firms' share price.

To break the short-term cycle, firms can take a proactive approach to attract long-term investors with patient capital. Presently, in many cases, this is done informally through investor relations activities. However, firms need to be more aggressive to extend this principle by offering financial incentives to investors who invest for the long term. Possible tools like the loyalty-shares (L-Shares) or the loyalty dividend could help to achieve this purpose. Both tools incentivize investors to hold shares for a more extended period, through the promise of an additional financial gain at the end of a contractually agreed upon period, which usually can be defined as multiple years. The application of loyalty securities or dividends in attracting and retaining patient capital promotes long-term investment horizons among investors and facilitates stability in financial markets. Utilizing loyalty-driven securities that are only paid to investors who have held stock for multiple years can play an essential role in promoting the mainstreaming of sustainable capitalism (Generation Investment Management 2012).

For the future direction, investors across the world, attracted by the advantages of green and sustainable investments, are seeking green bonds from financial and nonfinancial issuers. Although the green bond market is growing across the world, current corporate and financial sector green bond issuance remains comparatively small, which accounted for less than 5 percent of the existing $611 billion corporate green investments in 2017 (Figure 5.12).

Green bonds can be a critical tool for future corporate green investments and sustainable growth. In a free-market economy like the United States, the financial sector and large corporations have the collective power to allocate trillions of dollars of capital already in the system and can take the following approaches to significantly increase the power of green bonds:

- Revise game rules. To go beyond green bonds that specify the use of proceeds to "in or out" criteria at a firm level. If a company passes a credible test for being on an SDG-aligned path, then all finance it raises can count as green or SDG aligned.

This may result in lower financing costs for companies that meet investor demand for SDG-aligned and climate-proof solutions, creating a virtuous cycle of capital.

- Effectively utilize the capital market. Asset managers can raise funds via debt markets to allocate through their investment arms into superior-yielding green investments. Financial institutions with big green loan books ripe for securitization can recycle capital (Corporate Knights 2019).

Corporate green investment and the long-term investors in the capital market can create a win-win situation to mutually benefit from sustainable and low-risk return generated by firms with integrated thinking and reporting and following ESG metrics.

Conclusion

Free-market capitalism led by the United States has been a striking engine of wealth creation and economic growth over centuries. However, the rapid industrial growth proved to be unsustainable and is facing severe challenges, such as environmental degradation, the fragility of the financial system, inequality and populism, and the inadequacy of institutions, among which environment-related catastrophic climate change becomes one of the most immediate threats.

A possible solution to cope with the challenges is to rely on an effective free-market economic system that can allocate resources of financial, manufactured, human, intellectual, natural, and social capital in an accurate (to their best uses) and efficient (at the lowest possible cost) way. The corporate United States, especially large firms and financial institutions, can play a vital role in the process through integrated thinking and reporting, accelerated sustainable energy innovation, and corporate green investments, with support from government and nongovernmental organizations like Energy Information Administration, Committee for Economic Development, Generation Investment Management, and Corporate Knights.

The positive news is that U.S. firms continue to take the lead in the journey of sustainable capitalism in terms of corporate purchases of clean power (Figure 5.11), the number of sustainable companies in the Global 100 (Table 5.5), and total ESG investing assets (Figure 5.14).

Hope U.S. firms, asset managers, and investors can keep the momentum demonstrated in Figure 5.15 to promote the mainstreaming of sustainable capitalism via integrating ESG metrics in their long-term investment decisions as proposed by Gore and Blood (2011).

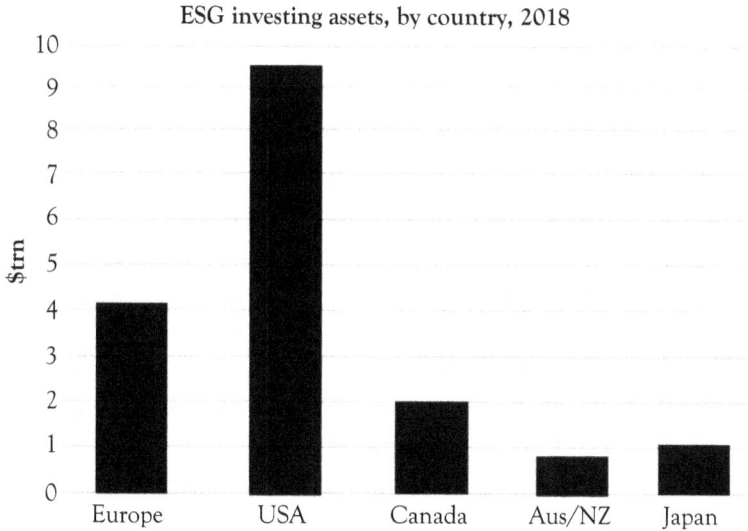

Figure 5.14 *ESG investing assets, by country, in 2018*[17]

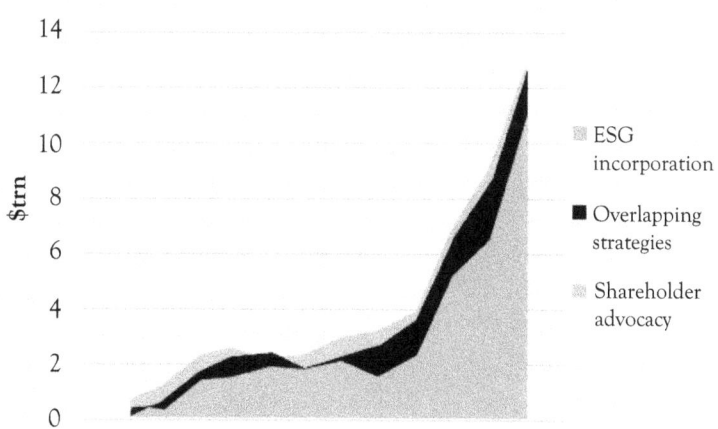

Figure 5.15 *Assets under sustainable management, United States, 1995–2018*[18]

[17 & 18] Sustainability Trends Report - 2019, by Generation Investment Management LLP. https://generationim.com/sustainability-trends/sustainability-trends-2019/

CHAPTER 6

Sustainable Capitalism and State Capitalism: China's Path

Overview

The U.S. model of free-market capitalism played a dominant force in the Cold War against communism, which set the agenda for economic governance and development until the financial crisis of 2008. The future of the world economic order becomes more uncertain with new challenges from alternative economic models, including models of capitalism adopting more state control as practiced in Brazil, Russia, India, and, especially, China. China is experiencing strong growth by embracing globalism and revamping the core principles of free-market capitalism. Meanwhile, the state still actively manages economic growth, including the deployment of industrial policy and financial and regulatory tools to foster industrial catch-up and technological development. China maintains state ownership of key enterprises, including the financial sector.

While China's so-called "state capitalism" practice certainly challenges the free-market status quo, it is worthwhile to examine whether such a path offers viable ways to organize capitalist production and market institutions, triggering any deviation in the global policy consensus (McNally 2013).

State Capitalism and China's Historic Remarkable Growth

SOE and the "Vertical Structure."

The term "state capitalism" has various meanings, but it is usually characterized by the dominance of a significant number of state-owned enterprises (SOEs) and active involvement in the employment of industrial policy and financial and regulatory tools by the state. Major emerging economies all experience some form of state capitalism, usually referred to as a hybrid system, in which the state is controlling an essential share of the economy while the private sector mainly operates in the free market.

In China, the market-oriented reforms started in 1978 and established a "socialist market economy with Chinese characteristics," which led to a fast expansion of the private sector, but SOEs remained an essential part of the economy. Li, Liu, and Wang (2015), through their research, proposed a "vertical structure" to describe a crucial unique feature of China's state capitalism. In such a "vertical structure," SOEs have monopolized key upstream industries, including financial, telecommunication, and energy sectors, and also have continually consolidated this power through management transfer and government-arranged mergers. Meanwhile, downstream industries include manufacturers of consumer goods, and service sectors, such as retailing, have been liberalized and mostly open to private competition. The key upstream sectors are still mainly controlled by the state, while the downstream industries operate under capitalism.

When competitive non-SOEs expanded due to productivity growth and factor accumulation in the market-driven downstream industries, it generated a higher demand for intermediate goods and services (such as energy and financial products) monopolized by the SOEs in those upstream industries. Therefore, even without any productivity and efficiency improvement, the upstream SOEs flourished more than the non-SOEs in the competitive downstream sectors through rent extraction. Furthermore, the enhanced trade liberalization symbolized by China's entry to the World Trade Organization (WTO) in

December 2001 created more external demand for the downstream tradeable, which ultimately enabled upstream SOEs to extract even more rents in the process of globalization (Li et al. 2015). "Vertical structure" offers a perfect description of China's unique state capitalism model. It also provides a good explanation of the rapid growth of Chinese economy without taking the U.S. type of free-market capitalism approach.

To examine closer China's "vertical structure," China's SOEs system is based on "vertically integrated groups" of large state-owned and related companies. Each group has a "central holding company," named the State-Owned Assets Supervision and Administration Commission (SASAC), which is the majority shareholder as a "core company" of the country. The individual group, in turn, owns a majority of shares in the state-owned companies that comprise the group, usually including a finance company that provides cash management and financing resources to group members. Altogether, these some 120 vertically integrated groups control SOEs that are all subject to government control via SASAC. According to Lin and Milhaupt (2011), total SOE assets accounted for 62 percent of China's GDP in 2010. There are also intragroup linkages via alliances, joint ventures, and cross-shareholding. Besides, the Chinese Communist Party (CCP) structure exists parallel to the "vertically integrated groups" structure. The Organization Department of CCP is decisive in selecting top executives of the SOEs, and in turn, some SOE executives hold positions in government and the CCP. Even the most prestigious senior executives of China's SOEs are cadres first and company men second, who naturally care more about pleasing their party bosses than about the market and customers. Besides, financial institutions controlled by the state also impact the SOEs through their financing resources, which are mainly loans from the state-owned banks in China. There are more than one chain of command from top to bottom as implied by this structure shown in Figure 6.1: "These hierarchical structures are embedded in dense networks—not only of other firms but also of party and government organs, and exchange and collaborate on many matters of production and policy implementation" (Lin 2017).

The implications of this system for a market competition run very deep. SOEs are generally exempt from antitrust enforcement. As the

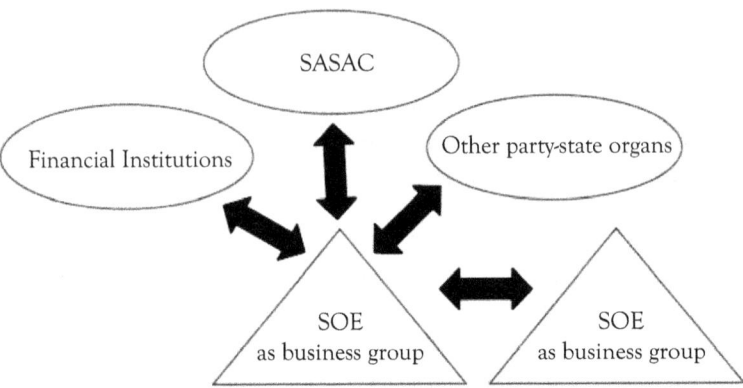

Figure 6.1 **A network anatomy of Chinese state-owned enterprises (SOEs)**[1]

Economist observed, the Chinese government "enforces rules selectively, to keep private-sector rivals in their place," and firms controlled by foreign capital can be blocked from acquiring local firms. The ongoing expansion of the state sector of China's economy limits the growth potential of the private sector. It also favors SOEs over foreign companies in some domestic markets (Lubman 2012).

It is vital to understand past, present, and future of China's "vertical structure" and many links between state ownership and the SOEs through "vertically integrated groups." Both have been playing critical roles in China's state capitalism.

World's Factory and Growth Powerhouse

Thanks to the unique "vertical structure" and China's access to the global market after the "Open Door Policy" announced in 1978, China experienced 10.2 percent annual growth rate averaged from 1983 to 2012 (Figure 6.2) and has become the world's second-largest economy next to the United States since 2010.

Having experienced a lengthy process of negotiations, China entered the WTO in 2001. Soon after that, from 2003 to 2007, China's exports

[1] Lin, L.W. 2017. "A Network Anatomy of Chinese State-Owned Enterprises." *World Trade Review* 16, no. 4.

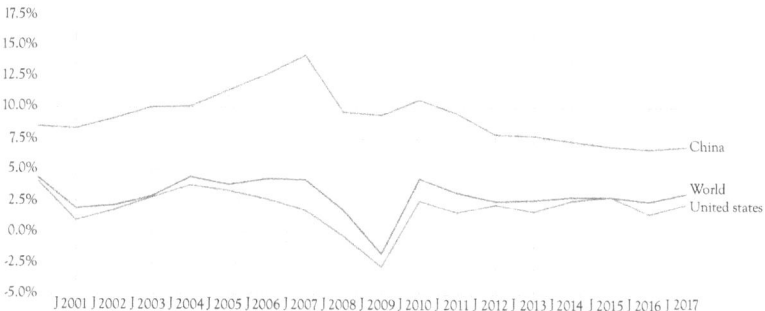

Figure 6.2 China's annual GDP growth from the year 2000 to 2017 compared to the world and the United States[2]

were growing at an annual rate of more than 25 percent, and in some years peaked at 35 percent. In 1990, China's exports accounted for only two percent of the world's exports and its manufacturing industry made up only three percent of the world's total. Less than two decades later, in 2017, China produced half of the global manufacturing output, and its exports jumped to 14 percent of the world's total. China surpassed the United States to become the world's largest international merchandise trader in 2013. After another two years, it replaced the United States as the top exporter in the world in 2015 (Figure 6.3) and won the name of the "world's factory" to reflect China's essential position in the global market (Cheng 2018).

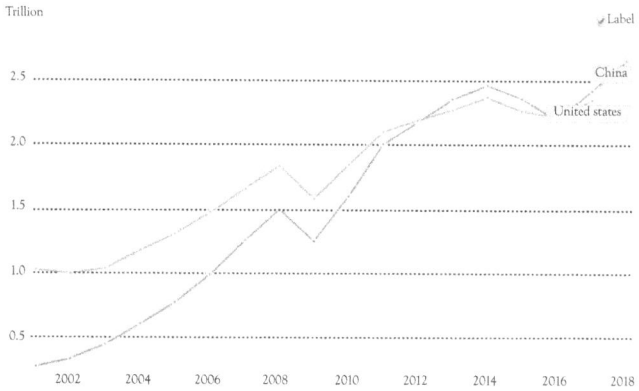

Figure 6.3 Exports of goods and services (current U.S.$). China has been in a rapid catch-up mode to surpass the United States since it joined the WTO in 2001[3]

---

[2] Data from World Bank. Last updated: July 6, 2018.
[3] World Bank national accounts data, and OECD National Accounts data files.

China has been viewed as the largest contributor and powerhouse of world economic growth since the global financial crisis in 2008. Recently, even its projected slower GDP growth remains impressive by the global and U.S. standards (Figure 6.2).

Rebalancing of the Economy with Challenges

China is entering a new chapter of its remarkable development story, undergoing an economic transition to slower but, hopefully, more balanced and sustainable growth. As Figure 6.2 demonstrates, China's GDP growth has been on course to gradually decline since 2010 as the economy went through structural adjustments toward a "new normal." GDP growth was at 7.8 percent in 2013, 7.3 percent in 2014, and 6.9 percent in 2015, indicating that growth has already fallen from the rapid growth period of 1983 to 2012 (World Bank Group 2017).

The future of China's "world's factory" is also facing uncertainty. Primarily, the "world's factory" was built upon its low costs to keep it competitive. However, these costs gradually and inevitably grew over time and weakened the country's fundamental comparative advantage to compete on a global scale. Through its "vertical structure," upstream-inefficient SOEs monopolized energy and financial sectors with higher prices to extract rent, both central and local governments imposed heavy taxes, and the strong exchange rate of the Chinese currency Yuan (CNY), all contributed to the rising costs.

The recent trade war between the two largest economies of the world, the United States and China, gives the "world's factory" another blow. China needs advanced technology for its manufacturing activities, but it can't solely rely on its own research and development. In the past, China resorted to forcing technology or intellectual property transfer or using illegal ways to get new technologies in a short amount of time, which became a cause of the U.S.–China trade dispute. The trade war will potentially lower Chinese products' market share in the United States. It may eventually result in the decline of China's status of the "world's factory" (Cheng 2018). China and its sustainability in the future are facing multiple challenges, especially in the following areas.

Limitations on SOEs' Rent Extraction Model

One side effect of China's "vertical structure" is that, although the strength of SASAC's control over the firms it oversees may vary in practice, insiders exercise control in each SOE, which causes fragile corporate governance. Shareholders have no control of the firms and no voice in corporate affairs and cannot access the courts in China. Limited transparency means that corporate misgovernment is easy to happen and conceal (Lubman 2012), which results in an overall lower return on assets (ROA) compared to private enterprises all the time. The gap has been widening since the 2008 financial crisis (Figure 6.4).

A recent economic transition with a much slower growth rate and external tensions would cause the "vertical structure" unstabilized. China's downstream private industries are losing the momentum due to the shrinking global market and disinvestment of foreign companies. They will be strangled by the upstream SOE monopoly and lose international competitiveness if upstream SOEs fail to lower mark-ups and improve productivity. Meanwhile, the rise of domestic wages endogenously to a high enough level with industrialization would only make things worse (Li et al. 2015). In reality, ROA of both China's state and private industrial firms started to decline after 2011 (Figure 6.4). SOEs

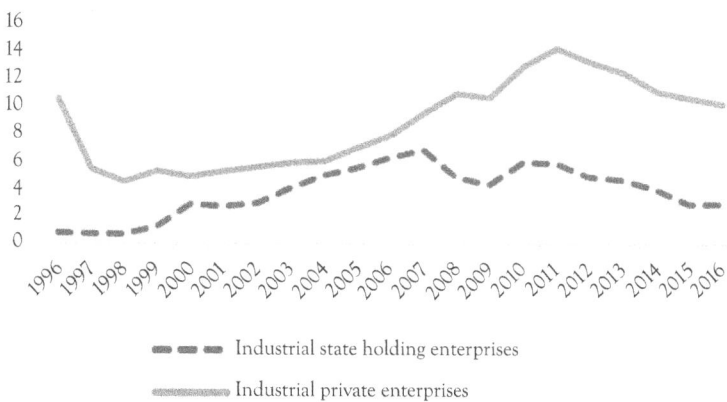

Figure 6.4 Return on assets of China's state and private industrial firms, 1996–2016

Source: China NBS

underperformed with much lower ROA (2.9%) versus private firms (around 10%) in the most recent years. Overall, the rent extraction model used to benefit upstream SOEs is hard to continue. However, based on the political considerations, China decided to strengthen the state control in its economy through "trustworthy" SOEs, which led to the recent increase of the share of SOEs' fixed-asset investment since 2015 (Figure 6.5), though SOEs' ROA kept decreasing (Figure 6.4). Both internal weakness and external threats make the sustainability of China's "vertical structure" debatable.

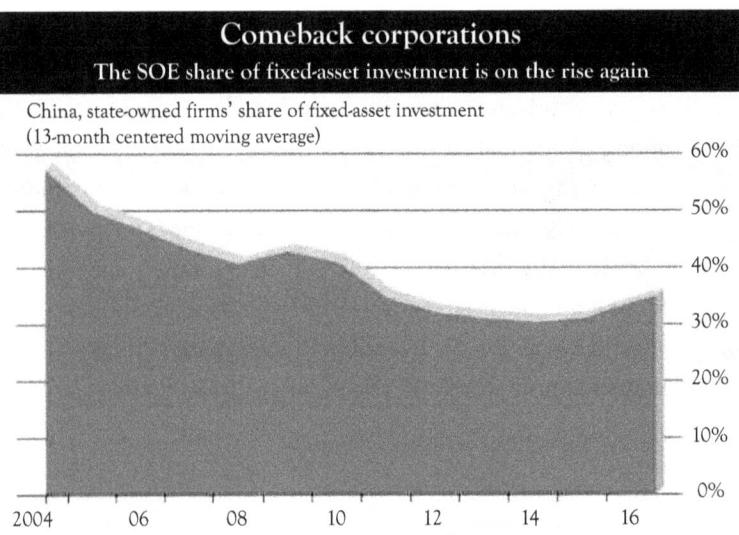

Figure 6.5 The SOEs started to increase their share of fixed-asset investment after 2013

Source: CEIC, The Economist

Environmental and Public Health Challenges

Another challenge is from the rapid growth of the "world's factory" itself. Manufacturers in the developed markets are expected to comply with specific basic guidelines concerning health and safety regulations, protection of the environment, and wage and hour laws. Chinese factories are known for not strictly following most of these rules and

guidelines, even in a permissive regulatory environment. Chinese factories have long shift hours, and the workers are not provided with proper
compensation and insurance. Some factories and construction companies even have policies where the workers are paid only once a year, a
way to keep them from quitting their jobs before the year is out. Environmental protection laws are routinely unenforced, especially when
local government weighs current tax income more than the long-term
environmental sustainability. Therefore, as a common practice, Chinese
factories cut down on waste management costs, which result in severe
air and water pollution. According to a World Bank report, 16 of the
world's top 20 most polluted cities were in China in 2013.[4] China's
CO_2 emissions (kg per PPP $ of GDP) in manufacturing and service
have been much higher than the world average and roughly double the
level of the United States, though it has been reduced significantly since
1990 (Figure 6.6).

China is also on top of the total CO_2 emissions list (Table 6.1), which
ranks as number one in the world and accounts for 27.2 percent of global
emissions and almost double the United States at the second place in
2017.

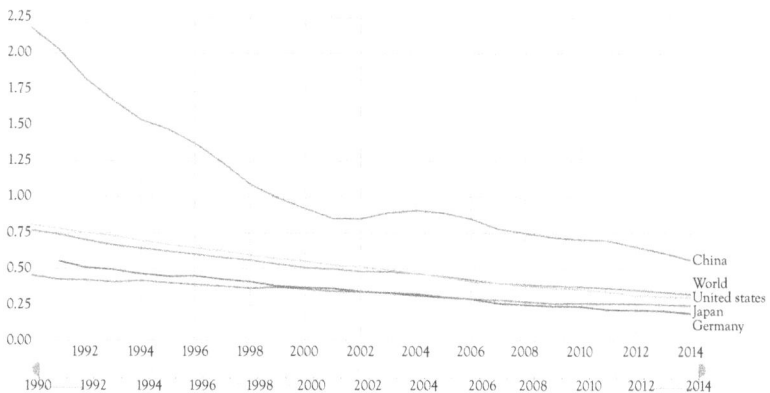

Figure 6.6 CO_2 *emissions (kg per PPP $ of GDP)*[5]

---

[4] https://investopedia.com/articles/investing/102214/why-china-worlds-factory.asp
[5] Data from World Bank. Last updated: July 6, 2018.

Table 6.1 Where most of the world's CO$_2$ emissions come from, sorted by country[6]

Rank	Country	Emissions in 2017 (MtCO$_2$)	% of global emissions
#1	China	9,839	27.2%
#2	United States	5,269	14.6%
#3	India	2,467	6.8%
#4	Russia	1,693	4.7%
#5	Japan	1,205	3.3%
	Top 15	26,125	72.2%
	Rest of World	10,028	27.7%

A direct consequence of such massive CO$_2$ emissions is its negative impact on air quality and public health. As shown in Figure 6.7, China suffered at an annual death rate of 117 per 100,000 population caused by

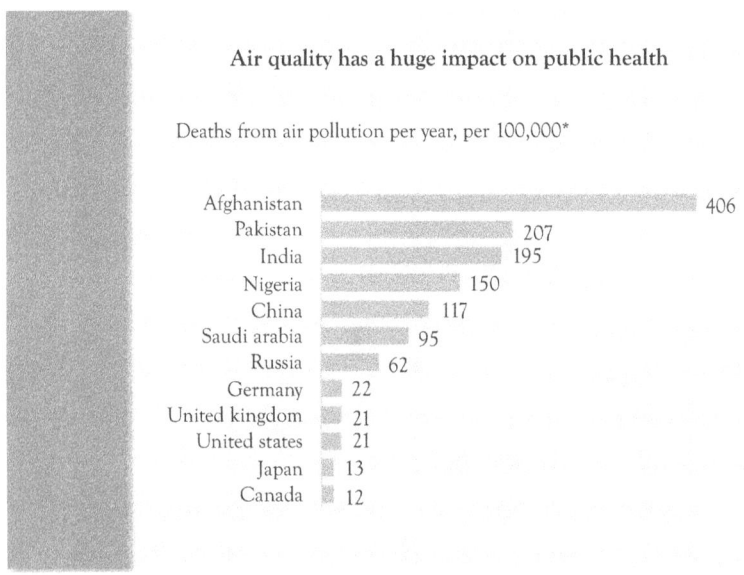

Air quality has a huge impact on public health

Deaths from air pollution per year, per 100,000*

Afghanistan	406
Pakistan	207
India	195
Nigeria	150
China	117
Saudi arabia	95
Russia	62
Germany	22
United kingdom	21
United states	21
Japan	13
Canada	12

* *Age-standardized, selected countries*

Figure 6.7 Air quality has a significant impact on public health

Source: World Health organisation; Statista; Health Effects Institute, State of Global Air 2018

---

[6] *Source*: Global Carbon Atlas (http://globalcarbonatlas.org/en/CO2-emissions)

air pollution in 2018, which put it on an embarrassing top five list despite its achievement as the world's second-largest economy.

Climate change resulting from CO_2 emissions is also anticipated to increase the risks of natural catastrophes. In fact, China is one of the countries most affected by natural disasters, especially earthquakes, drought, and flooding, and its poor and vulnerable are disproportionately hurt because they often live in high-risk areas (World Bank Group 2017).

The environmental challenge becomes a top priority issue on China's current agenda and becomes a direct threat to its future development.

Capital Investment and Financial Distress

Financial resources are indispensable to cope with the challenges of SOEs' "vertical structure" and the environmental threat that China is facing. Unfortunately, China's investment-driven growth model makes its overlevered financial market itself another big challenge. There are risks from China's significant stock of accumulated debt and the possible growth in recent years due to a disorderly deleveraging of the economy. The increase in corporate and local government leverage in China since the global financial crisis in 2008 has been hasty (Figure 6.8). The lessons learned from other emerging markets suggest that such rapid rises in the credit-to-GDP ratio are often ensured by slower economic growth and potential financial crisis. The slowing economic growth, the piled-up corporate and local government debt, the decline in corporate profitability, and ROA, together with overcapacity in specific sectors, have raised concerns about the overall credit quality in China (World Bank Group 2017).

Furthermore, China's economic growth is expected to drop more due to the lower contribution from labor as China's working-age population is expected to decrease. Also, total factor productivity (TFP) growth is expected to be lower as the massive reallocation of resources, including labor, within the economy is expected to decline. China will need to transform to a new growth model based on advanced technology and higher productivity, which will require reversing the declining contribution to growth from TFP (Figure 6.9). The projected TFP growth could

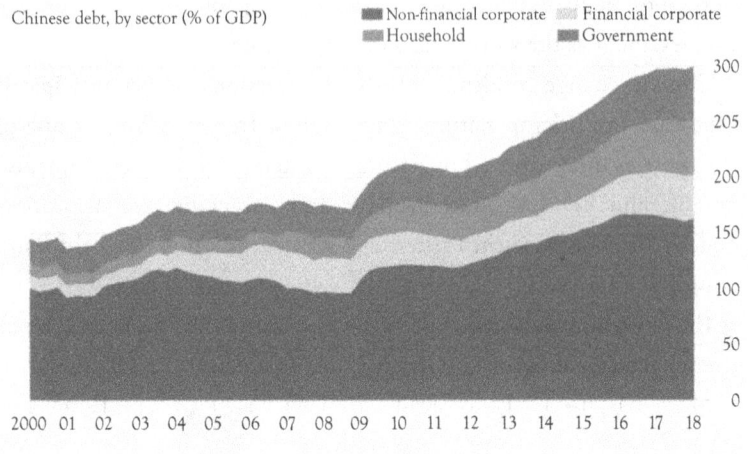

Figure 6.8 China's gross debt exploded to almost three times its GDP with the biggest increase in the nonfinancial corporations[7]

Source: IIF © FT

remain relatively high by international standards, depending on the extent of structural reforms that promote market competition and upgrading of technologies (World Bank Group 2017).

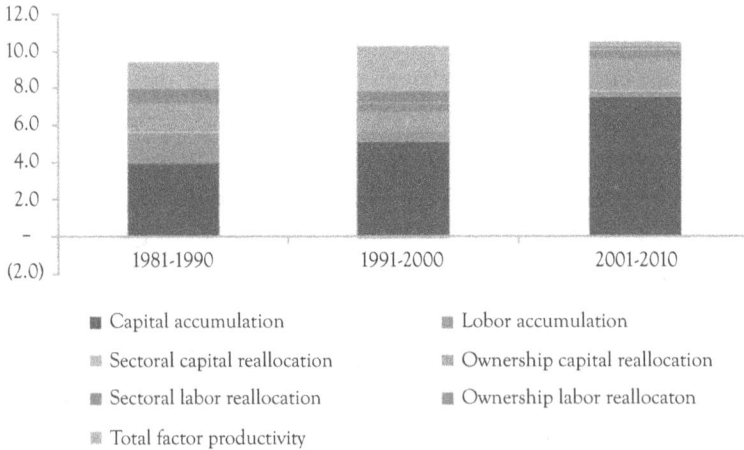

Figure 6.9 Growth accounting for China

Source: World bank Calculations and China NBS

---

[7] https://ft.com/content/0c7ecae2-8cfb-11e8-bb8f-a6a2f7bca546

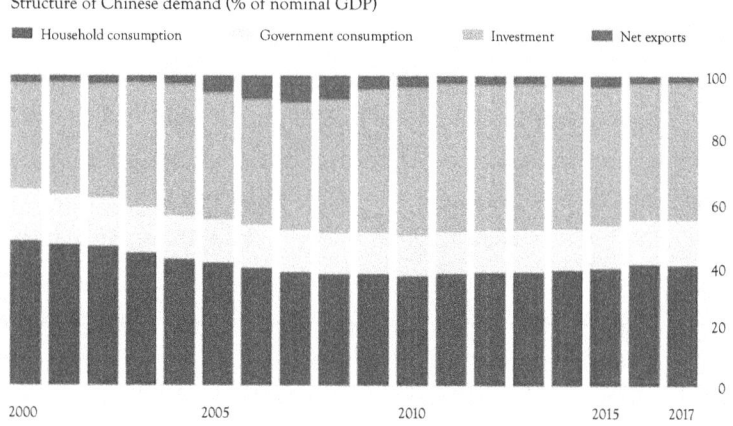

Figure 6.10 China's demand became even more dependent on investment[8]

Source: Haver Analytics © FT

However, China's GDP growth is still heavily reliant on capital invest-ment (Figures 6.9 and 6.10), which is, by far, the number one driver of its economic development. The investment-driven model would only make things worse to increase financial distress and create a dilemma for the already over levered situation.

"New Normal" and "Green Growth"

To respond to China's tough challenges, the Chinese government, with the vast resources under its control, is supposed to play the most critical role in developing new strategies. In May 2014, President Xi Jinping intro-duced the term "New Normal" to describe an economy with lower but more efficient and equitable growth. The specific path of "New Ideas, New Thoughts, New Strategies on State Governance" are reflected in China's 13th Five Year Plan (FYP) 2016–2020. In order to transit to the "New Nor-mal," the state is committed to promoting innovation and further open-ing up structural reforms, streamlining bureaucracy, implementing stricter

---

[8] https://ft.com/content/0c7ecae2-8cfb-11e8-bb8f-a6a2f7bca546

environment protection, and delegating power and resources to lower levels of governments.

To deal with the sustainability concerns, the Chinese government comes up with another solution called "Green Growth," which can be defined as maximizing economic growth and development while stopping rising trends in natural resource use, CO_2 emissions, and environmental degradation. Clearly, the government seeks a transition to green growth with lower greenhouse gas emissions. "New Normal" and "Green Growth" emphasized by the 13th FYP for 2016 to 2020 reflects a shift in China's growth model from the "world's factory" to pursue high rates of return while promoting environmental sustainability and making investments in "greening" growth (World Bank Group 2017).

World Bank Group (2017) also offered its own solution and issued *The Systematic Country Diagnostic (SCD) for China* identifying the key challenges and opportunities for China to achieve the "Twin Goals of ending extreme poverty and boosting shared prosperity in a sustainable manner." Table 6.2 provides a summary of China's SCD prepared by the World Bank Group.

Table 6.2 China's Systematic Country Diagnostic (SCD) priorities and potential reforms identified by the World Bank Group[9]

SCD Priorities	Potential Reforms
Manage the transition to a slower but more balanced and economically sustainable growth.	• Structural reforms may require accepting slower growth now to establish the basis for a more balanced and sustainable growth in the future. • Promote market competition and the private sector by reducing market constraints and ensuring level playing fields. • Address the significant stock of debt in the financial and corporate sectors. • Strengthen local government fiscal and debt management capacity, including by enhancing fiscal transparency. • Promote greater innovation in the economy, including by strengthening intellectual property rights, expanding basic research, and helping firms strengthen their managerial capacity.

---

[9] Source: World Bank Group. 2017. *China - Systematic Country Diagnostic: Towards a More Inclusive and Sustainable Development.*

SCD Priorities	Potential Reforms
Address the economic and social instability that may result from the economic transition.	• Address the economic and social losses that may result from the industrial restructuring planned by the government, through targeted temporary income support, active labor market programs, and robust social security programs.
Reduce the disparity in access to quality public services.	• Address remaining barriers to migration by continuing to reform the hukou system to reduce the bias against migrants in urban areas. • Make the intergovernmental fiscal systems (transfers) more progressive, and rebalance the intergovernmental allocation of revenues and expenditures. • Address the large disparities in public spending on education to equalize education opportunities for the poor, including for early childhood education, and implement a quality assurance system. • Improve the availability of affordable quality health care in rural areas and strengthen health insurance for the poor. • Provide stronger incentives and enhanced supervision for local governments to focus on service delivery, beyond the current dominant focus on investments and growth.
Improve farm productivity and efficiency in rural areas, thereby reducing the income gap with urban areas.	• Establish more efficient and sustainable climate-smart agricultural production systems with green ecology–oriented agricultural subsidies. • Promote rural land transfers, greater farm scale, and the specialization and professionalization of agricultural operations. • Promote the application of new technologies, such as information communication technologies and ecommerce platforms, to the agriculture sector.
Make fuller use of market mechanisms to promote green growth and more efficient, sustainable use of natural resources.	• Continue to pursue market reforms to promote competition in the energy markets and expand the use of market instruments to manage pollution and climate change. • Strengthen the focus on environmental sustainability in the cadre management system, including by clarifying the acceptable tradeoffs with economic growth. • Adjust resource and energy prices, including the tax regime, to fully reflect environmental costs. • Mobilize private sector financing and encourage private sector participation in pollution cleanup and restoration. • Strengthen the governance and institutions for the environment, including with regard to the monitoring and enforcement of environmental laws and regulations. • Improve the availability of critical environmental information.

"New Normal" and "Green Growth" as the state-level strategies set a clear tone for China's future path toward sustainable development under state capitalism.

Ongoing SOE Reforms with More Determined Directions

In state capitalism, the future direction of the "vertical structure" is vital to the success of China's new sustainable development strategies. In November 2013, CCP, the actual decision maker of the state, after affirming the continued importance of SOEs in the economy to provide public goods and promote strategic industries, including natural and financial resources, military security, and technology, announced the transformation of China's SOEs as part of a wide-ranging economic and social reform program in the following areas:

1. Boosting efficiency and commercial orientation. The announced SOE reform plans highlight ownership diversification and the reorganization of state-owned capital investment and operating companies. According to the announcement, government functions of SOEs would be separated from enterprise management, and numerous state-owned capital investment companies and operating companies would be established by founding new entities and regrouping existing ones. In July 2014, the SASAC, which supervises the central SOE groups, announced that six SOEs had been selected for a pilot program to deepen mixed-ownership reform, to increase private ownership in SOEs.

2. Ensuring a more level-playing field. In China's transition to a more market-driven economy, it will take well-designed and implemented actions to ensure a level-playing field, which would put greater competitive pressures on incumbent firms, including SOEs, to raise their productivity. In China, a level-playing field means fair and transparent treatment between enterprises with or without state ownership. Relevant reforms could include requiring a market rate of return on state equity capital and removing perceived government-implicit guarantees of SOE borrowing. It could consist of equal access to land, natural resources, and government subsidies

as well as equal treatment in regulations, tax, government procurement, and administrative approvals. As part of this effort, in 2016, the State Council issued an opinion on the establishment of a fair competition review system, which mandates competitive assessment of policy measures and scrutiny of monopolistic conduct by the Anti-Monopoly Law.

3. Establishing a sound modern corporate structure and corporate governance. The mixed-ownership reform is expected to increase the role of private stakeholders in SOEs and is designed to increase the transparency of the decision-making process and improve management skills at the executive level.

The overall direction of SOE reform is moving toward a more market-driven model with diversified ownership to raise capital and improve corporate governance. Meanwhile, how successful can China reform its SOEs while maintaining SOEs' upstream position in the "vertical structure" is worth further observation.

Take the Lead on Renewable Energy

To deal with the urgent environmental threats, as a commitment made at the state level, China's Nationally Determined Contribution (NDC) targets a cut in the country's CO_2 emissions per unit of GDP by 60 to 65 percent from 2005 level by 2030.

Based on World Bank estimates, China already spends approximately 1.2 percent of its annual GDP on environmental protection each year, mostly on industrial pollution. China is anticipated to reduce environmental degradation and resource depletion by six percent of gross national income (GNI) by 2030, which indicates a significant improvement (World Bank Group 2017). Such a large scale of investment surpassed any countries and regions in the world in 2013 and reached its record high of $132.6 billion in 2017 (Figure 6.11), which resulted in the development of renewable energy in China attracting global attention in recent years.

As another critical effort of CO_2 emissions reduction, electric and plug-in hybrid vehicles are growing fast, with a current global fleet of 5

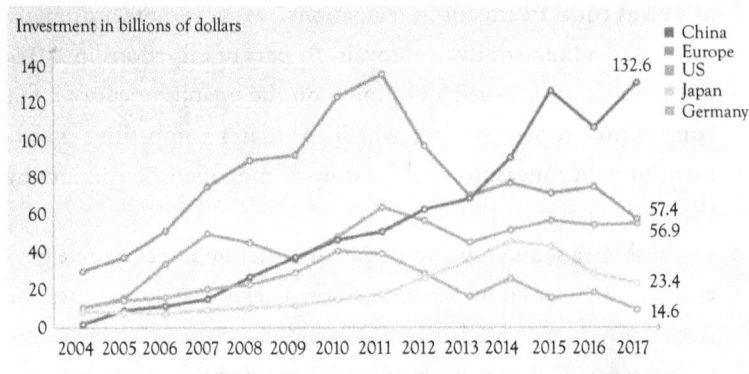

Figure 6.11 China takes the lead on renewable energy in terms of total investment

Source: Bloomberg New Energy Finance

million battery electric vehicles and plug-in hybrid cars as of 2019. Again, China has led the world with its number of electric and hybrid vehicles delivered since 2016. In 2018, its electric and hybrid a concise deliveries were roughly four times the United States (Figure 6.12).

At present, China also leads the world renewable energy production in terms of wind and solar power capacity. With large-scale industrial applications, renewable energy costs have fallen substantially. Looking at the history of photovoltaic (PV) technology: the price of PV modules decreased from about 30 Yuan (Chinese currency) per watt in 2007 to about 10 Yuan in 2012, and further reduced to just 2 Yuan by 2017. In 2012, China's installed

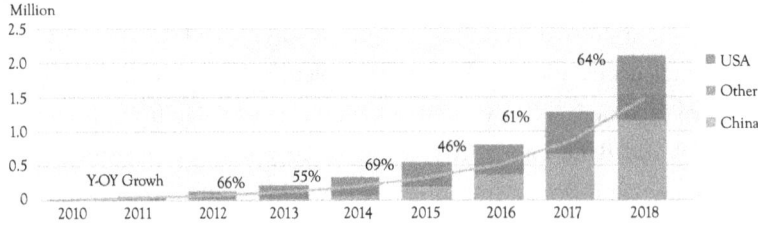

Figure 6.12 Global plug-in deliveries of BEV and PHEV[10]

* BEV, battery electric vehicle; PHEV, plug-in hybrid car. The chart refers to light vehicles.

---

[10] Source: ev-volumes.com

capacity of solar and wind power was only 3.4 GW and 61 GW, respectively, while the annual electricity generated by renewables was 2.1 percent of China's total consumption. By 2017, China's solar and wind power capacity increased to 130.06 GW and 168.5 GW, respectively, and the share of renewables was growing to 5.3 percent of China's electricity supply.

The successful development of China's renewable energy fully illustrates the effectiveness of China's approach to on-grid tariff subsidies offered by the government. The on-grid tariff policy, through which the government can make renewable energy production more competitive and attractive to businesses and investors, shows its advantage to anchor the revenue of power generation throughout the entire life cycle. By taking China's approach, government subsidies convey a clear price signal to investors and can adequately support the early-stage development of renewable energy (Lin 2018).

State capitalism demonstrated the advantage of its capability to put in huge investment and subsidies with support from the state government and achieve astounding results in a very short period in addressing environmental issues with effective solutions, such as electric vehicles and renewable energy.

Debt-to-Equity Swap and Green Investment

Overlevered excessive debts burden the Chinese financial system as a serious threat that the Chinese government has labeled as one of its "three critical battles" (which refer to the battles against major risks in the Chinese economy, the other two named poverty and environmental pollution) to sustain economic growth and stability. Utilizing its unique strength of state capitalism, the Chinese government developed a plan to slow the growth of new lending and reduce the existing bank loans through multiple approaches that include the debt-to-equity swap program.

In the debt-to-equity swap program, not only the state-owned banks but also more private enterprises are getting involved as equity investors in some heavily indebted state-owned enterprises to reduce their debt ratio. The share of executed swaps involving private firms, though still relatively small as 6.5 percent of all signed swap contracts (24 of the 367 signed contracts) in April 2019, significantly grew from 1.2 percent (1 of 81 signed contracts) at the end of September 2017.

According to the recent data released by the State Council, the swap program has expanded in scale since 2017. By the end of April 2019, 40 percent of the signed swap deals by value have been executed. It indicates good progress in the swap program, which is a leap forward from 14 percent at the end of 2017 (Figure 6.13).

According to the State Council's *Opinions on Vigorously, Steadily and Properly Reducing Corporate Leverage Ratios* announced in October 2016, besides the debt-to-equity swap program, the following approaches are listed as primary tools to address the high leverage issue:

1. Promoting mergers and restructuring of enterprises;
2. Modernizing corporate governance and strengthening self-regulation;
3. Revitalizing existing corporate assets;
4. Optimizing debt structure of enterprises;
5. Implementing corporate bankruptcy; and
6. Expanding equity financing.

Again, with intervention from the state, a set of tools are implemented to address the challenge of excessive debt. Although the latest data shows

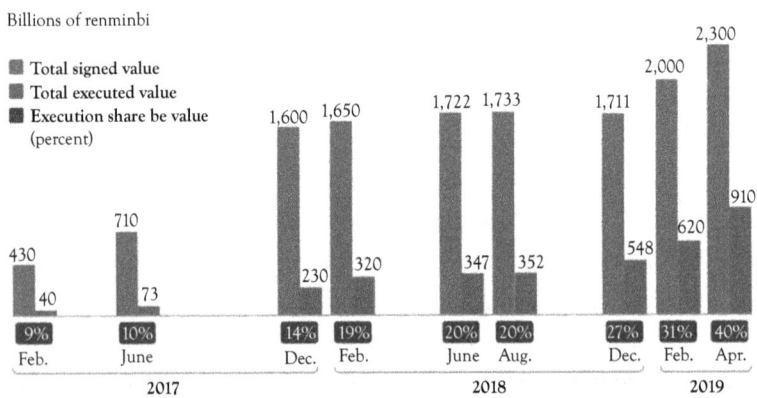

Implementation of China's debt-to-equity swap program is improving

Figure 6.13 Implementation of China's debt-to-equity swap program from 2017 to 2019

Source: State Council of China: National Development and Reform Commission of China; China Banking and Insurance Regulatory Commission

that China's implementation of the debt-to-equity swap program has improved, the program has done little to curtail the overlevered situation. China is constrained by its policy of not letting market forces play a truly decisive role in pricing the swaps. Without such a capability, the Chinese government and its swap program may still not be able to win this chosen battle (Huang 2019).

Besides its effort of deleveraging the economy, a new direction of capital investment initiated by the Chinese government is "The Belt and Road Initiative (BRI)," which was proposed by China in 2013. BRI is expected to mobilize tens of trillions of dollars for much-needed infrastructure development in emerging market economies (Figure 6.14). According to the World Bank, approximately 70 percent of global greenhouse gas emissions come from the construction and operation of infrastructure, which includes power, transportation, and buildings. As the BRI-related countries will host most of the world's new infrastructure constructions in the coming decades, if the Paris Agreement goals are to be reached, it is crucial that these projects are green and low carbon.

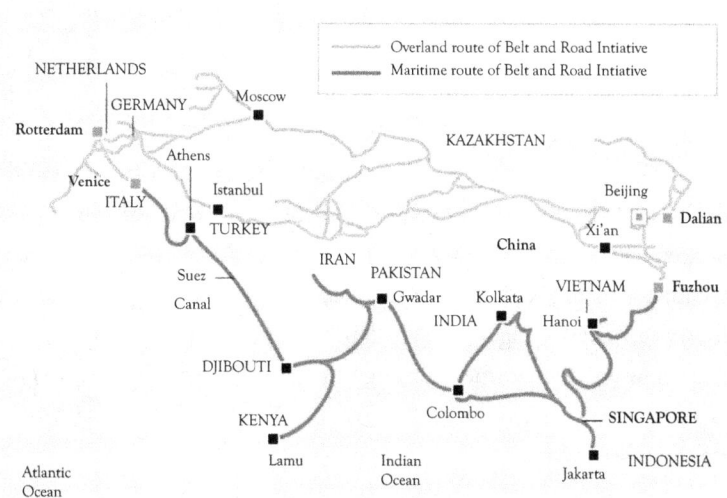

Figure 6.14 The Belt and Road Initiative involving infrastructure development and investments in Asia, Europe, Africa, and the Middle East[11]

---

[11] Source: Straits Times.

In November 2018, the Green Finance Committee of China Society for Finance and Banking and the City of London's Green Finance Initiative jointly launched a set of voluntary principles, the Green Investment Principles (GIP) for the BRI. Other significant contributors to the drafting of these GIP include the World Economic Forum, UN-supported Principles for Responsible Investment network, the Belt and Road Bankers Roundtable, the Green Belt and Road Investor Alliance, and the Paulson Institute. The GIP document calls for lenders, investors, and corporates that invest and operate in the BRI region to ensure the projects they invest are aligned with the requirements of the Paris Agreement and environmental sustainability. The GIP proposed to incorporate ESG metrics into the corporate governance of related firms. Recommended practices include utilizing green financial instruments, measuring and releasing environmental and climate information, and adopting green supply chain management.

As of the end of June 2019, 29 global institutions, including all major Chinese banks engaged in the BRI countries and some of the largest financial institutions from the related nations, have signed up to the GIP. By doing so, the signatories are fully committing to sustainability and demonstrating their ESG responsibility for the emerging world. The GIP will also create a win-win situation by bringing benefits to its signatories and supporters, giving them better access to innovative green investment products and opportunities for cofinancing green projects in the rapidly growing BRI region and best practices in environmental and climate risk management (Jun 2019).

China is using its state-controlled resources to fight two battles at the same time to deleverage through debt-to-equity swap program and to make a new green investment through the BRI. Both are hard to imagine and have very little chance to be successful without the strength of its state capitalism system.

Conclusion

As a fast-growing emerging economy, China is facing similar yet unique challenges in its path toward sustainable development. China attempts to cope with its challenges with a system different from free-market capitalism adopted by the United States. China has been implementing a "socialist market economy with Chinese characteristics," which, indeed, is a state capitalism system in which the state is actively managing economic growth and capital and resource allocation.

China developed its unique "vertical structure" benefiting SOEs and, recently, "New Normal" and "Green Growth" strategies to explore its way of sustainable capitalism under state control. It managed to make some progress, especially the impressive ones in electric vehicle deliveries and renewable energy production.

It may look like China has a way out. However, it is still too early to judge whether China's state capitalism path is a better approach leading toward healthy prosperity and sustainability over the long run.

CHAPTER 7

The Role of Business Schools: Criticism and Legitimacy

Introduction

Over the last two decades, business schools have been exposed to a lot of criticism supporting mainstream economic and business model even when things got out of hand. But some have claimed that this is only understandable since business schools are also businesses that belong to the same business model as the rest of the global economy. They have become big business with a surprisingly little evaluation of the impact of business schools on either their graduates or the profession of management (Pfeffer and Fong 2002) with two immediate consequences. First, the criticism that possessing an MBA degree or the grade earned in the courses does not correlate with career success, and second, about the little evidence that business school research is influential on management practice, which calls into question the professional relevance of management scholarship. Authors like Hambrick (1994) and Pettigrew (2001) find business school research seldom relevant and actionable. Likewise, Khurana (2007) and Adler and Harzing (2009) have emphasized that business schools have sold out to the tyranny of rankings.

Martin pointed out that focus in business schools was on narrow functional knowledge acquisition instead of a broad issue-centered approach embracing business and society as embedded in a plurality of context. Others criticized business schools' focus on disciplinary knowledge acquisition instead of the development of an interdisciplinary and integrated perspective (Khurana 2007). Such discussion all came at the expense of development of critical thinking of business students. In many situations, they do not develop their capability to ask essential questions and understand severe conditions or learn that organizations are rational and logical and then discover later about complexities of the same (Datar et al. 2010). Such dilemma for students results in a persistent knowing-doing gap (Colby et al. 2011) whereby students must acquire knowledge while there are a little room and possibility for them to practice what they have learned. Knowledge and technical skills must guide their professional judgments. But it also needs to be based on ethical sensitivity concerning public expectations and values related to the issues and decisions.

As such, they would miss and have a distorted focus on the importance of values and ethics in business (Ghoshal 2005; Khurana 2007), causing them to be reduced to managers, or agents of shareholders, dedicating their careers to the sole purpose of creating private wealth. Such a role, in effect, tends to strip them from any professional identity, self-respect, and personal responsibility, also leaving them unprepared to cope with challenges of roles, responsibilities, and purpose of business in society (Gentile 2010; Swaen et al. 2011, Bieger 2011). This educational attitude and profile are also connected with the legitimacy of business school research, which rarely addresses societal issues. It also seldom informs on important policy questions relating to the issues like public education, poverty, or sustainability (Dyllick and Muff 2016. Likewise it reveals its inability or no willingness to inform society and policy and contribute to the common good, not just to do good for the few private actors as recent financial crisis revealed (Rynes and Shapiro 2005).

A Lack of Legitimacy

A lack of legitimacy of business schools, for the aforementioned reasons (and more!), has been developed as one of the leading issues and core of the research on the potential of their future development. The legality of business schools came under renewed scrutiny following the corporate scandals at the start of the millennium and ensuing financial crisis (Hommel and Thomas 2014). One layer of legitimate criticism is related to the allegedly instrumental, amoral, and selfish vision of human behavior that lies behind much of the modern managerial theory and training (Ghoshal 2005; Mintzberg 2004; Mitroff 2004; Pfeffer and Fong 2004). The other is related to the fact that humanity-based training has been largely squeezed out of business schools' curriculums (Bennis and O Toole 2005; Duncan 2004; Starkey and Tempest 2009; Wright 2010).

A lot is at stake here. The birth of the new business model is apparently not a matter of minor importance. Henisz (2011) proposes a somewhat central thesis to reform related to the reinstitution of business school's legitimacy stating that such reforms are stuck because they threaten relationships with existing stakeholders while being ignored in current measures of business school's performance. He stresses the fact that change is possible but only if enlightened internal leadership and pressures and resources from civil society, government, students, and employers successfully frame their calls for reform. Also, it is essential that such improvements tap into deep-seated concerns about neoliberalism in economic policy making more broadly and form an unlikely alliance to triumph over entrenched faculty, disciplinary paradigms, and short-term financial constraints.

Potential for Substantial Changes

Authors and scholars have also assessed potential for substantial changes in what business schools research and teach (Willson and Thomas 2012) and focusing the need for the new business model by addressing various themes, including but not limited to the broadening of the traditional focus of research and teaching to look more broadly to broader society; embracing multidisciplinary perspectives; turning its theoretical perspectives and research focus toward big questions; engaging in public and policy debates; reclaiming the terrain of work, employment, and society; placing greater emphasis on the ethical and moral questions endemic in modern capitalism; critically examining the role of business and managers in society; asking big questions about development; becoming less insular and nationally oriented and understanding language; comparative social cultures and impact of religion on global economic activity.

In that context, business schools would be able to respond to societal issues related to sustainability agenda also as belonging to these big questions of current state economics and business (Boyle 2004; Schoemaker 2008). So far business schools' research has basically excluded contributions to some of the most significant problems societies are facing, the decarbonization of the economic system, and bringing the resource consumption within the constraints of the planet, which needs an interdisciplinary and transdisciplinary approach.

Earth preserving, people-centered, and deleveraging of economic value creation are only some of the features of newly sustainable capitalism in the making where efficiency and effectiveness as core values of business making are complemented by the principle of sustainable with wide-ranging implications from local to international level. The United Nations started three decades ago to develop this new bold vision of a sustainable economic model. Should business schools champion this process in responding structurally to the global need for the creation of unique or adapted business and economic value?

That is the reason our research seeks to re-energize the discourse around sustainable capitalism. We believe it is necessary to refine our arguments and thus make a stronger and even more persuasive economic case. We seek to do our best to reach and win over the *you-will-need-to-convince-me* group, which consists of those open to persuasion on the business rationale for sustainability.

Recently business school education researchers started to emphasize the importance of the systemic introduction of sustainability agenda into business school's curricula as part of management education (Hommel et al. 2012). But the situation is far from ideal since there are still many real barriers to integration of sustainability to core management disciplines in the format of the proposed new global business model (Rasche et al. 2013). Sterling (2004) outlines three possible levels of response regarding adoption of sustainability agenda or education about sustainable capitalism in the system of higher education. He distinguishes educating about sustainability (and classifies it as an accommodative response), educating for sustainability (listing it as a reformative response), and finally education in the format of capacity building (as a transformative response).

Sustainable Capitalism Education

During research for this book, we were inclined to propose all three approaches discussed here in the matter of challenging the sustainable capitalism agenda and in introducing the new business model: from education about it till building capacity for it. Presently most of the sustainability relevant education in business schools is of an incrementalism kind and uses an incrementalism reform approach addressing critical global sustainability issues, and yet, there is demand for more transformative sustainability results in management education (Starik et al. 2010).

Another avenue of modern business school education on sustainability is done in a piggybacking form of integration of sustainability within existing structures (Lamsa et al. 2008). Piggybacking means that sustainability agenda is added to individual sessions of courses or modules inviting guest lecturers to speak of corporate social responsibility (CSR) and sustainability, but some have criticized this approach for integrating sustainability into the curriculum in a no uniform manner (Rusinko 2010).

There are different forms of an introduction of a sustainability agenda into management education. When teaching sustainability as soft skills (Truscheit and Otte 2007) teamwork and conceptualizing an argument are addressed as the sustainability principle. Developing sustainability literacy (Stibbe 2009), on the other hand means indicating the skills, attitudes, competencies, dispositions, and values that are necessary for surviving and thriving in the declining condition of the world in ways that slowdown the decline as far as possible. Sustainability in business schools can be included across the whole curriculum, adding interdisciplinary perspectives (Roome 2005) but also as systems thinking, which is one of the major blocks in sustainability thinking (Clayton and Radcliff 1996; Stibbe 2009). When educating about sustainable economics and sustainable capitalism besides systemic approach, authors emphasize the need for a holistic, systemic understanding of the new business model (Baets and Oldenboom 2009, Werhane and Painter-Morland 2011). A holistic, systemic understanding is thus critical to responding to sustainability agenda. In a complex system, the interaction between cause and effect is dynamic and nonlinear; multiple factors work together complexly to trigger change.

Henceforth, a business school as an open system theory of education about sustainability agenda has been proposed (Painter-Morland 2011). These education modules influence those within it and the knowledge they generate and deliver but are also affected by other external dynamics. The curriculum does not develop independently from the business school system or business, environment, and society. It is the cause and effect of systemic change and stakeholders' involvement, meaning a significant systemic institutional integration of sustainability in business school's missions (Painter-Morland 2015), which builds on a systemic capability toward sustainability and elaboration of the new business model. The aforementioned is distributed and nurtured more throughout organizations which create impetus toward change in students, faculty, administrators, institutions, as well as the organization that hire its alumni. This then requires a higher emphasis on connectedness (Leroy et al. 2001, Courtice and Van der Kamp 2013), namely on the need to connect education to business, society, and natural environment. Finally, it addresses sustainability in a manner of capacity building for sustainable economies and business models (Burchell et al. 2015; Akrivou and Bradbury-Hung 2015), empowering institution members to effect change and ensure a transformative social context.

The neoliberal model does not appear on track to form the basis of the extended 21st century or even as is the case with the regulatory state half a century (Henisz 2011). New business models must adjust to that fact. Some of the neoliberal models most notably generated crisis including the financial crises of the mid and late 1990s in Latin America, East Asia, and Russia accelerating through the collapse of the dotcom bubble; accounting scandals of Enron, World Com, Parmalat; and finally, the global financial crisis of 2008–2011.

As compared with the economic liberalism of the 19th century, neoliberalism enjoys a similar hegemonic status supported by numerous coercive intermediary actors (Henisz 2011). It diffuses globally because the academic theory was available and backed by powerful national and international actors, but also because public policy makers have confronted inflation, unemployment, debt crisis, and other systemic failures often linked to politically motivated intervention in their economic systems in the 1980s of the last century. Henisz stresses the fact that the rise of neoliberal economics came as a response to a systemic crisis of regulatory economics. Namely, the postwar gold standard collapsed under the strain of war on poverty and war in Vietnam, exchange rate volatility. Monetary policy responses further complicated government regulations, price pressures from labor, and commodity suppliers toward inflation. Financial markets and corporations have responded to new uncertainty and tension by globalizing production and seeking to hedge national exposures. This combination of events contributed to an investment boom in emerging markets, increasing international capital flows, which in turn increased the leverage of global forces. Opinions regarding the appropriate policies on national economic policy making and fiscal policy couldn't any longer be focused on maintenance of aggregate demand at a level consisting of full employment and price stability. Exchange rate stability and financial system stability were at various points in time, and in many markets, the prime focus of government policy makers eager to maintain credit or investment.

Today many assume that the current model will be replaced by the surge of the protectionist regulatory system of the second part of the last century, as being witnessed by the current administration in the United States. It is easy to see why historical pendulum could swing in that direction. The focus of governmental policy in centrally planned or regulatory-based economics (Johnson 1971) has changed from the center of the liberal finance of the 19th and first quarter of the 20th centuries which targeted the enhancement of the efficiency of markets. In emerging economies, and especially frontier markets, the goal was industrialization, which it was argued would free the peripheral countries from their dependence on the core. The role of government in the market economy was no longer indirect, setting the foundation in which economic activity could take place, but rather a direct action, undertaking the pursuits that would attain and maintain full employment, instead of ensuring the invisible hand could operate, policy makers optimized against constraints.

Development economics evolved around the enlightened leadership of economists who first calculated the investment gap needed to regain the convergent growth path and subsequently, the human capital and policy gaps. The presumption has always been that well-intentioned economists, guided by theory, could engineer progress better than at an unregulated market (Henisz 2011). It is reasonably natural to assume why, from this point on, there was a call to return to governing economics, which to many can be very appealing. It addresses some of the main features of the crisis of the present model, inequalities in economic growth, technology, and wealth, as well as low level of utilization of national economic factors, expressly high level of unemployment.

But managing state economics is not equal to sustainable capitalism since this model could also create, as it has historically done, a separate set of pressures on human, environmental, and financial resources of all economic, social, and environmental agents included. Likewise, one of the reactions toward the current neoliberal model is what one could name "greening business as usual," which is also not a sustainable version of capitalism, but the current model with some of the greening language and outlays.

Some authors have analyzed the differences between the mainstream economic model, so-called green growth, and sustainable well-being (Constanza et al. 2012), to emphasize its crucial differences. As for the primary principle of production or creation of economic value, the mainstream neoliberal model is focused on producing more, with minimal involvement of government and with no influence of external costs of prices of its products and services measuring success only regarding marketed financial values created and with emphasis on private properties. The misallocation of capital in the past two decades has contributed to the manifestation of several concurrent crises: climate, biodiversity, energy, food, and water, as well as the global financial and economic crisis. In response to these systemic crises, the UN has stressed the need for a shift to a more sustainable and inclusive economy, reached by adequately incorporating social and environmental policies in development planning.

This green model presents a kind of transition mode toward sustainable capitalism, also called sustainability well-being. The principal purpose of green economy policies and investments is, therefore, dual: first, to create new and more sustainable physical capital, human capital, and social capital; and second, to maintain, enhance, and rebuild natural capital as a critical economic asset and source of public benefits. Protecting natural resources, from clean freshwater to forests and air, is especially important for poor people who depend on these resources for their livelihoods and are especially vulnerable to environmental contamination and degradation. Unlike the current mainstream economic model, sustainable capitalism recognizes poverty as an essential phenomenon and is focused on reducing it through a variety of involvement with green sectors.

Regarding the preservation of natural capital, the green growth model recognizes its importance in any model of valuation and allocation of resources and the course of regulatory instruments and government intervention aimed at the preservation of such capital. Finally, sustainable well-being model is centered on the principle of the better in the economy, society, and nature. Besides financial indicators of success, a variety of human welfare indicators related to environmental and social dimensions have gained prominence.

Fighting poverty becomes the prominent role of sustainable capitalism, where the government plays a significant role in facilitating and brokering new strategies. Besides natural and social capital, the principle of public property institution becomes a prominent mean to secure the overall functioning of this system. The challenge is how business schools embedded in their current trends, practices, and values can interact with the business establishment in a more sustainable model of capitalism.

CHAPTER 8

Sustainable Capitalism in the Business School Curricula

Introduction

The world today is changing rapidly and profoundly, economically, and politically, as well as socially, while capitalism is under siege (Porter and Kramer 2011). We believe, therefore, that it has become more important than ever to educate business students in this changing environment, where scholars and academics, as well as practitioners, must recognize how crucial for business today is the idea of sustainable capitalism and development. By sustainable development, we mean development that "meets the needs of the present without compromising the ability of future generations to meet their own needs" and includes at the same time the three pillars of economic, social, and environmental development (WCED 1987).

Currently, almost 30 percent of the students worldwide who pursue undergraduate and/or graduate degrees enroll in higher education business schools (AACSB 2017). In the United States, for instance, business and management education is the largest single field in higher education, due in large part to the result of institutional rankings and statistics that show the future economic value of a degree in business. Such potential for economic payback, however, is not an automatic guarantee of the quality of the graduate's education.

Business Schools Curricula Development

In today's general debate about business school curricula development, one criticism, in particular, has received significant attention, that the greatest world problem of our time is sustainability with its environmental, economic, and social implications. The debate has initiated the third shift in business school education (Starkey *et al.* 2004; Giacalone and Thompson 2006; Bradfield 2009; Thomas and Cornuel 2011) and in the business itself (Porter and Kramer 2011; Scherer *et al.* 2013). As a result, it has become necessary to rethink the purpose and justification for business school education. Some scholars (Porter and Kramer 2011) call for a revolution in society supported by business entities and business schools in which the focus is on both societal and organizational rationality. Hence, many business schools have come to the realization that they must adapt their management education to meet the changing societal and economic demands for responsible resource stewardship, offering a business education with both scientific rigor and societal relevance (Holland 2009).

Business Schools and Society

Our society seems to have changed its attitude toward environmental problems, as in many countries, predominantly in Europe, more environmental legislation is being passed, such as the new emission standards in the automotive and transportation industries. As a result, hitherto undreamed of environmentally friendly product improvements have been manufactured. Various other actions that reflect environmental and safety concerns have also been taking place, such as Germany's announcement that it will close all its nuclear power plants by the year 2022.

It has further been suggested, by the European Communities that gross domestic product (GDP) as a measure of the market value of goods and services could be replaced with a measure of human welfare that takes into consideration the sustainability of future production (European Communities 2009). Such a change, which may very well turn sustainability the *business* solution of the future, is consistent with the opinions of some of the most well-known management thinkers of today (Porter and Kramer 2011).

Across the Atlantic, protests by the Occupy Wall Street movement have drawn attention to the perils in the current financial system and perhaps in the entire world order, as discussed in Chapter 1, which suggests that a paradigm shift in the attitude toward capitalism may be evolving. Assuming it takes place, the impact of such changes on business and employees is difficult to predict.

Somewhat different recommendations have been made in the hope that global wealth will still continue to increase. Acs and Phillips (2002) argued that society is best served by an "entrepreneurial capitalism" that relies on volunteerism, private foundations, and "giving back to society," along the lines of philanthropists such as Rockefeller, Soros, Turner, and Gates. Other scholars suggest there is a need for more "social entrepreneurs" (Seelos and Mair 2005; Martin and Osberg 2007), such as OneWorld Health (United States), Sekem (Egypt), or Grameen Bank (Bangladesh).

As far as the promotion of, and instruction in, sustainability issues in business school curricula, a significant challenge is to change peoples' and institutions' general "economic-ideological" ideas and principles. From the perspective of green ecologists, sustainability means radical changes are required if the world is to survive (Hudson 2005). From this point of view, business schools, with their support of materialism and capitalism, are the enemy. If radical changes as argued by Hudson were implemented, the logic behind the business model that most business schools still promote would lose its support and legitimacy.

However, there is a second and opposing perspective that maintains that technological solutions within existing means of production offer the promise of a trade-off between economic goals and environmental or even social objectives (Hudson 2005). What if the market is, in fact, the prime and best mechanism for efficient resource allocation, as argued by the Austrian school of economics? In such case, business schools could maintain their status quo by continuing to teach the same curricula and the same economic models. This would be business as usual, with no paradigm shift necessary. In fact, Harvard Business School's Professor Robert Simons (2013) argues that business schools have become part of the problem rather than the solution, as these institutions are not focusing enough on what *the business of the business* actually is, namely, to restore a focus on competing to win. This is the traditional focus of market capitalism.

There is yet another viewpoint, which lies somewhere in between these two extremes. Proponents of such perspective accept the general legitimacy of markets as mechanisms for resource allocation, but they admit the need for nonmarket, state regulation, suggesting that business schools should play a vital role as go-between institutions that mediate between the market and the state. Looking at the current trend, at least in the west, it appears that this intermediary role may appeal to many academics and higher education institutions, as it is a role that is advantageous to them. Al Gore, former U.S. vice-president, Nobel Peace Prize laureate, and environmental activist, shares this view, recommended at a seminar at University of Gothenburg (October 2010) that business schools teach "sustainable capitalism" as the path to the maximization of long-term economic growth, which would require the integration of environmental, social, and governance issues with business strategies, risk assessments, and, not least, reward systems.

Sustainable Capitalism in Business School Curricula

BizEd, one of the prominent magazines in business education in the United States, is an advocate of socially responsible business. The magazine and its publisher, AACSB, are currently investing much time and effort in promoting business sustainability. It is evident that more business schools are now addressing sustainability issues. For example, in 2007, Bloomberg *BusinessWeek* published the Aspen Institute's alternative ranking of MBA programs (at 111 institutions, of which 71 are in the United States). On average, the business schools ranked in the survey offered six electives dedicated to social and environmental issues in their curricula, which was an increase of one elective since the previous inventory is taken two years earlier. Of the schools, 63 percent required students to take a course on "business and society issues," and 35 percent offered a unique concentration in social and environmental issues.

Perhaps somewhat disappointing. However, the same report states that there are few sustainability topics in the core courses of business schools. The schools surveyed said that professors discussed such issues in only five percent of core accounting courses and only one percent of core finance courses. Unfortunately, not much has changed since 2007. A 2012 ranking by the same institute of 82 top U.S. business schools stated that "many programs offer little or no course work" in the area of green business and sustainability (Gloeckler 2013, p. 1).

One reason for the lack of sustainability issues in business school curricula is that university lecturers often do not have a clear understanding of sustainability (Reid and Petocz 2006). For many lecturers, it seems easier to define nonsustainability than to define sustainability; therefore, they often continue to use business model failures from the past as pedagogic examples. The problem is exacerbated by the fact that many business students are unaware and uninterested in these issues (Reid *et al.* 2009). Thus, among lecturers and students, there is a great deal of uncertainty, even ignorance, about the meaning, scope, boundaries, application, and limitations of the term sustainability that a more explicit definition might resolve.

Pfeffer and Fong (2004, pp. 1516–1517) argued that business schools should place greater emphasis on their professional ethos and "break free of the rating game and vocational focus that constrains their ability to provide critical analytic thought and analysis." They state that the business model for business schools must include a real-value proposition that promotes innovative ideas and ideas about the profession of management educators, about management, and about business life in general, all in the context of the sustainable society. Such positions, however, seem to be somewhat more ideological than practical, as the concept of sustainability need not be contrary to the concept of making money.

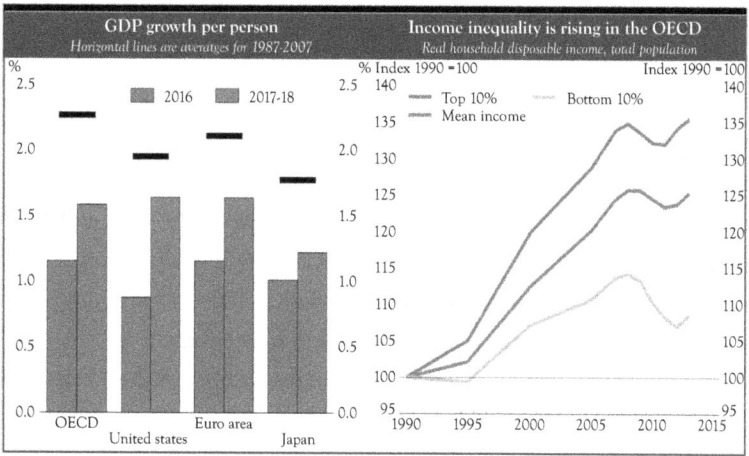

Figure 8.1 GDP growth per person is below history, and income inequality continues to rise

Source: OECD June 2017 Economic Outlook database and OECD Income Distribution Database
Note: RHS is the unweighted average of 17 OECE countries.

Thinking in terms of money-making alone instead of thinking in terms of sustainable capitalism seems narrow-minded and fairly old-fashioned, though. Indeed, several Harvard Business School faculty (Bower *et al.* 2011) recommend that CEOs work in the interests of more stakeholders and take a more active role in trying to overcome global threats to capitalism itself, including but not limited to inequality, global warming, corruption, and weaknesses in the world's financial systems, as depicted in Figure 8.1.

Short-Termism and Quarterly Capitalism

Prominent business leaders have begun to talk about the crisis caused by the continued use of yesterday's business models in practice. For instance, the managing director of McKinsey & Company, Dominic Barton, is a critic of what he calls "short-termism and quarterly capitalism" and an advocate of "long-term capitalism" (McKinsey 2011). He argues that continued growth and a flourishing economy are only possible if we learn to live within rational financial and ecological constraints. He is not alone, as several CEOs of well-known market capitalists support such views.

Paul Polman, the CEO of Unilever, states that incentives connected to short-term reporting are at the heart of today's financial problems. He contends there must first be an alignment between the capital's interests and capitalism. Roger Ferguson, president, and CEO of TIAA-CREF, the large institutional investor, believes the system is more in error than its people (McKinsey 2011). Undeniably though, systems, in the same way as business models and institutions, are only created, maintained, and changed by people. While new possibilities, such as those stemming from significant innovations, technology advancements, and globalization, have created more economic value, ecological and social constraints, however, necessitate that future business models deal not only with possibilities but also with societal boundaries and restrictions.

Current awareness in business circles is that companies need help with their business models if they are to integrate and manage sustainability (Arevalo *et al.* 2011). Peter Bakker, the new president of the World Business Council for Sustainable Development (WBCSD), calls for a "new operating system" for capitalism that can "break the lock of business as usual." He maintains that action and implementation are needed because, for 40 years there has only been a talk (WBCSD 2012). However, this "revolution of capitalism" (pp. 6–7), as he calls it, requires that sustainable performance be "concrete, measurable, comparable, and linked to the scientific priorities."

The Role of Business Schools: A Society with Sustainable Capitalism

There are several factors influencing the internal and external factors of integration of sustainability issues in business school curricula, and in business practices, to outline the required change in existing curricula to support sustainable capitalism. In our views, many researchers, academicians, practitioners, and students recognize sustainable development as a critical issue in the contemporary business environment and in higher education. Work in the discipline is in progress with evidence of some satisfactory results (Slater and Dixon-Fowler 2010). Although sustainable development has a high profile in some disciplines, in some respects, sustainable development remains a marginal concern in other quite influential disciplines.

Educators and researchers are often role models for students. This is as true in the area of sustainable development as in more traditional areas of instruction. Business school professors best fulfill this role when they share real-life stories from their professional and consulting experience, problem-based learning, close cooperation with businesses in the development of sustainable business models and cross-discipline courses (Teece 2010), and a holistic approach to education (Bennis and O'Toole 2005; Giacalone and Thompson 2006; Bradfield 2009; Thomas and Cornuel 2011). Besides interest and commitment, professors need special pedagogical skills for this complex task. Consensus policies regarding the need for increased funding for professors, especially for course administrators, are also indispensable. As more students request sustainable development courses, there must be a pool of knowledgeable professors qualified to present these courses. In addition, the administration should be open to change in the curricula. If only the enthusiasts support such change, there is less chance of success. Strong administration commitment is needed to gain the interest and trust of the students.

Responding to the external pressure to be a "modern business school" and to have an "up-to-date" curriculum must resonate with the inclusion of sustainable themes and issues in the curricula. It should be a requirement for business schools that compete for reputation and research funding, as well as for students. We believe that every business school should include sustainability in its business modules. We are convinced that the demand for graduates educated in sustainable capitalism will increase as its business relevance becomes better known. In addition, we would argue that it is the responsibility of business schools to train its researchers to study sustainability issues using a curriculum that emphasizes academic rigor and relevance.

The development of course materials, therefore, should satisfy the demands of students, businesses, various other stakeholders, and the general public, which can be very time consuming, especially if the school were to implement sustainability across all curricula, which will require rigorous course and curricula reviews, coordination of the various disciplines, and education and training of professors. In addition, the role business school should have in raising awareness of the mission and vision related to sustainability issues, as well as defining the strategies necessary to implement the mission and vision, is not an easy undertaking. One practical issue, for instance, would be whether students should have the opportunity to make their own selection of sustainability courses. The alternative is to offer them programs with required sustainability courses. This administrative issue sometimes has the unfortunate effect of overshadowing the more strategic issue, which is informing new students about the mission and vision of sustainable capitalism.

A major issue business schools face when implementing sustainability in their curricula is the fact that scientific knowledge and practical application of sustainability in the workplace are also not well developed. Severe problems arise because of the complexity of the supply and demand between business schools and businesses and because of the uncertainty about whose needs and demands to focus on and how. Ideology has a powerful influence as far as the proposed solutions to these. These are crucial questions for business schools that cherish the independence that is the right of institutions of higher education. In the best of the higher education worlds, such changes should be pioneered, and change is driven in response to society's demands, but only to the extent that academic freedom is not compromised. Hence, business schools should be ahead of best practice in the business world, taking charge of the revolution. The increased complexity of the business environment means that discipline-based curricula are increasingly unable to capture all the elements needed to understand and manage real-life problems (AACSB 2011, 2013). In part, this explains why business schools, in many cases, seem to lag behind the fast-changing world of work.

In summary, free-market capitalism is an economic philosophy that has, more than any other, benefitted humankind in many places worldwide. This should not be forgotten in the discussion about the future role of business schools. Much of the empirical research suggests that when business school leaders and course administrators/professors commit enthusiastically to education in sustainability issues, the opportunities for a conversation about sustainable capitalism increase significantly. Business schools ought to realize that they have an obligation to integrate issues of sustainability in their programs and curricula because the return on financial capital alone is not an adequate measure of success: social and natural capital must be included. Teaching the concepts behind sustainable capitalism means preparing leaders and managers for the future and demonstrating that success is measured not only by the amount of profit but also by how the profit is earned.

Global Sustainable Capitalism Principles for 21st Century

As discussed throughout this book, the recent global financial crisis of 2007/2008 has raised widespread concern for the sustainability of the global economy, and much has been written concerning the negative impacts of economic development on natural ecosystems and civil societies. Unfortunately, few viable alternatives to the prevailing economic paradigms have been suggested for consideration. Those that have been are typically little more than suggestions for fine-tuning capitalist or socialist economies.

In his highly recommended book *The Essentials of Economic Sustainability*, John Ikerd addresses the basic principles and concepts essential to economic sustainability. Some of these concepts are capitalist, some are socialistic, and others are general principles validated by philosophy or common sense.

The following is a list of principles for sustainable global capitalism. None of them are unique in nature, with some being addressed by Ikerd, others appearing in the mainstream media, or discussed in the chapters of this book.

The following are 11 global sustainable capitalism principles to consider:

1. **Unsustainable capitalism:** Unsustainable capitalism is largely related to the crisis of neglect for nature and human capital. Do not disregard, *kick the can*, or attempt to reinvent human and the earth. Instead, strive to preserve and enhance the goals and values of your business. There is no fundamental contradiction between sustainable development and capitalism, Capitalism 2.0 that is. As Jonathon Porritt argues in his book *Capitalism as if the World Matters*, we should not seek to replace capitalism with a better, fairer, and more ecologically friendly economic system. We must continue to develop Capitalism 2.0, for the various advantages it presents compared with other systems.

2. **Unsustainable capital:** Such a form of capital becomes unable to meet its long-term commitments and disfavor long-term investments. Do not neglect the long-term dimension of your business and regenerate and communicate as much as possible a long-term contribution of your business stakeholders, making economies viable from local to global levels. As we argued throughout this book, there is a fundamental contradiction between a profit-oriented economic system and long-term environmental sustainability. Often, the solutions offered by mainstream environmental economists as well as their ecological economy colleagues do not solve the central problems but serve to further highlight the difficulties of changing Capitalism 1.0 to 2.0, sustainable capitalism. In a profit-oriented economy, capital accumulation is a prime driving force, and nongrowth for the economy at large tends to result in serious economic and social crises. On the other hand, a decoupling of economic growth from resource

depletion and environmental degradation is possible only within certain sectors or product types and within relatively short-term perspectives. The assumptions of mainstream economists about infinite economic growth (and infinite dematerialization) represent a false ontology according to which the powers and mechanisms of the natural world are considered totally controllable by humans as if they were mere epiphenomena of the human world. On the other hand, the assumptions of certain ecological economists about the possibility of steady-state capitalism disregard the relation between capital and surplus value, which constitutes a strong mechanism driving the capitalist economy toward limitless growth.

3. **Avoiding global unsustainably merges:** For sustainable business expanding internationally, being global is not more important than being small and local; many successful sustainable businesses are and will be small and local. Any crisis of global scale operations should be hedged by being present locally as well as globally.

4. **Being indeterminately more effective and efficient is not the final goal to increase value and grow a business:** Being sustainably effective and efficient is also related to trust, quality, and relationships build-ups with all who take part in all cycles of your business.

5. **Consider social and environmental outcomes:** Not only financial results and market share acquisitions matter in business. Considering social (the community, the shareholders, and stakeholders), environmental, and sustainable business practices are becoming increasingly important under Capitalism 2.0.

6. **Sustainable business requires sustainable customers local and abroad:** Business is long-term financially sustainable and client's/customer's incomes are also long-term locally and globally financially sustainable. Under sustainable capitalism, the focus on debt-driven operations is no longer a sustainable option for global Capitalism 2.0.

7. **A sustainable business model is a diverse model:** Sustainable business model is generically a diverse model, not one of convergence. There is not a major or ultimate business, or economic model, as its success will require sustainable calibration. Sustainability is not antiproductive. Instead, it is the ability to change and adapt related resources of productivity and creation.

8. **Sustainable capitalism involves transparent accountability:** It requires reporting on social, environmental, technological, and financial impact and results of business capital and operations.

9. **Growth of sustainable business is related to creation and maintenance of social and environmental justice:** Without a sustainable peace, mutually fulfilling and meritocratic values for groups and individuals, there will not be a business success under Capitalism 2.0.

10. **Sustainable capitalism is being characterized by flexible currency and money exchange:** The postmodern world of finance is directly correlated to diversity, and the multitude of conventional and electronic money and currencies exchange, globally and locally, and is more about payment transactions and less about financial asset investments. Are you prepared for it?

11. **Sustainability is about the reinstitution of economic responsibility:** As much as it is about deepening of true economic freedom. Sustainable capitalism fosters freedoms of economic self-determination on all levels of the economy.

Conclusions

Contemporary Chinese artist Ai Weiwei observed that "Liberty is about the right to question everything." This empowering statement reminds us that those who have the ability to question the status quo should cherish the privilege and make their voices heard. Only through collective discourse are we able to advance, by refining or even completely changing key tenets of our society. Similar to the way artists often draw inspiration from challenging times, perhaps companies and investors can use the global financial crisis, and global warming, as a catalyst to reshape how we view the world and to foster positive change.

The barriers to mainstreaming global sustainable capitalism are formidable but not insurmountable. We believe that the actions for change we are recommending, taken together, will affect the entire business ecosystem and encourage reform by investors, companies, government, and civil society alike to adopt long-term horizons and consider ESG factors in addition to financial ones.

These actions will also drive the development of solutions for our sustainability challenges. By this we mean not only investing in assets using an integrated sustainability methodology but actively funding projects and companies that are developing the solutions to sustainability challenges themselves (e.g., smart grid infrastructure service firms, low-income housing developers, and affordable life-saving drugs).

According to Tim Jackson, the Economics Commissioner on the UK Sustainable Development Commission, "Questioning growth is deemed to be the act of lunatics, idealists, and revolutionaries. But question it we must." The exercise of reflecting on the sustainability of current business practices and developing ways to improve going forward requires us to revise our views on the nature of the value we create, the type of expansion we seek, and how we measure success.

Incremental change will prove insufficient to mainstream global sustainable capitalism by 2020. So, like an artist at the easel, our goal is not to make superficial touch-ups that conceal deep structural flaws beneath. We are calling for a fresh canvas on which, together, we can paint a new picture of our future.

References

AACSB. 2017. Available at: http://aacsb.edu/-/media/aacsb/publications/data-trends-booklet/2017.ashx?la=en, last accessed on 03/02/2018

ACCA., and IMA. 2016. *From Share Value to Shared Value: Exploring the Role of Accountants in Developing Integrated Reporting in Practice*. Retrieved July 12, 2019, from https://imanet.org/insights-and-trends/external-reporting-and-disclosure-management/share-value-to-shared-value?ssopc=1

Acs, Z., and R. Phillips. 2002. "Entrepreneurship and philanthropy in American Capitalism." *Small Business Economics* 19, no. 3, pp. 189–204.

Adler, N.J., and A.W. Harzing. 2009. "When Knowledge Wins: Transcending the Sense and Nonsense of Academic Rankings." *Academy of Management Learning and Education* 8, no. 1, pp. 72–95.

Akrivou, K., and H. Bradbury-Huang. 2015. Educating Integrated Catalysts: Transforming Business Schools Toward Ethics and Sustainability." *Academy of Management Learning & Education* 14, no. 2, pp. 222–240.

Antunes, D., and H. Thomas. 2007. "The Competitive Disadvantages of European Business Schools." *Long Range Planning* 40, no. 3, pp. 382–404.

Arevalo, J., I. Castelló, S. de Colle, G. Lenssen, K. Neumann, and M. Zollo. 2011. "Introduction to the Special Issue: Integrating Sustainability in Business Models." *Journal of Management Development* 30, no. 10, pp. 941–954.

Baets, W., and E. Oldenboom. 2009. *Rethinking Growth: Social Intrapreneurship for Sustainable Performance*. Palgrave Macmillan.

Bennis, W.G., and J. O'Toole. 2005. "How Business Schools Lost Their Way." *Harvard Business Review* 83, no. 5, pp. 96–105.

Bevan, D., and P.H. Werhane. 2011. "Stakeholder Theory." In *Business Ethics and Continental Philosophy*, eds. Mollie Painter-Morland and René ten Bos, 37–60. Cambridge University Press.

Bieger, T. 2011. "Business Schools–From Career Training Centers Towards Enablers of CSR: A New Vision for Teaching at Business Schools." In *Business Schools and their Contribution to Society*, eds. M. Morsing and A. Sauquet Rovira, 104–113. Sage, London.

Block, F. 2007. "Understanding the Diverging Trajectories of the United States and Western Europe: A Neo-Polanyian Analysis." *Politics & Society* 35, no. 1, pp. 3–33.

Bower, J.L., H.B. Leonard, and L.S. Paine. 2011. "Global Capitalism at Risk: What Are You Doing About It?." *Harvard Business Review*. Retrieved from https://hbr.org/2011/09/global-capitalism-at-risk-what-are-you-doing-about-it

Bower, J.L., B.L. Herman, and L.S. Paine. 2011. *Capitalism at Risk: Rethinking the Role of Business*. Boston, MA: Harvard Business Review Press.

Boyle, M.E. 2004. "Walking Our Talk: Business Schools, Legitimacy, and Citizenship." *Business & Society* 43, no. 1, pp. 37–68.

Bradfield, S.L. 2009. "The Value of Sustainability Education." *Journal of Management Education* 33, no. 3, pp. 372–375.

Burchell, J., S. Kennedy, and A. Murray. 2015. "Responsible Management Education in UK Business Schools: Critically Examining the Role of the United Nations Principles for Responsible Management Education as a Driver for Change." *Management Learning* 46, no. 4, pp. 479–497.

Cassidy, J. 2010. "Interview with Richard Posner, Eugene Fama, John Cochrane and Gary Becker." *The New Yorker*, January 12, 13, 14.

Cheng, X. 2018. "The Fate of China's 'World's Factory'." Retrieved July 8, 2019, from www.theepochtimes.com website: https://theepochtimes.com/the-fate-of-the-worlds-factory_2690836.html

Clayton, A.M.H., and N.J. Radcliffe. 1996. *Sustainability: A Systems Approach*. London, Environment scan.

Colby, A., T. Ehrlich, W.M. Sullivan, and J.R. Dolle. 2011. *Rethinking Undergraduate Business Education: Liberal Learning for the Profession*. San Francisco, CA: Jossey-Bass.

Committee for Economic Development. 2016. "The Challenge of Sustaining Capitalism." May 2016 Update. Retrieved July 7, 2019, from Committee for Economic Development of The Conference Board website: https://ced.org/reports/the-challenge-of-sustaining-capitalism-may-2016-update

Corporate Knights. 2019. "Global Corporate Green Investment and the UN Sustainable Development Goals." Retrieved July 8, 2019, from https://corporateknights.com/wp-content/uploads/2019/03/2019_Corporate_Green_Investment.pdf

Costanza, R., S. van der Leeuw, K. Hibbard, et al. 2012. "Developing an Integrated History and future of People on Environment (IHOPE)." *Current Opinion in Environmental Sustainability* 4, no. 1, pp. 106–114.

Courtice, P., and M. van der Kamp. 2013. "Developing Leaders for the Future: Integrating Sustainability into Mainstream Leadership Programmes." Working paper of the Cambridge.

Csaki, G. 2009. "A Nemzetközi Valutaalap és a világgazdasági válság, 2008–2009 [The International Monetary Fund and the global economic crisis]." *Pénzügyi Szemle* Volume LIV, pp. 545–567.

Datar, S.M., D.A. Garvin, and P.G. Cullen. 2010. *Rethinking The MBA. Business Education at the Crossroads*. Boston, MA: Harvard Business Press.

David, C.W., T. Howard. 2012. "The Legitimacy of the Business of Business Schools: What's the Future?" *Journal of Management Development* 31, no. 4, pp. 368–376.

Dichev, I. D., J.R. Graham, C.R. Harvey, and S. Rajgopal. 2013. "Earnings Quality: Evidence from the Field." *Journal of Accounting and Economics* 56, no. 2, pp. 1–33. https://doi.org/10.1016/j.jacceco.2013.05.004

Dillon, J. 2003. *The Heirs of Plato: A Study of the Old Academy*. Clarendon Press.

Donella H.M., L.M. Dennis, R. Jorgen, and W.B. William III. 1972. *The Limits to Growth*. New York, NY: University Books.

Duncan, W.J. 2004. "A Case for Great Books in Management Education." *Academy of Management Learning & Education* 3, 421–28.

Dyllick, T., and K. Muff. 2016. "Clarifying the Meaning of Sustainable Business: Introducing a Typology From Business-as-Usual to True Business Sustainability." *Organization and Environment* 29, no. 2, 156–174. https://doi.org/10.1177/1086026615575176

Dyllick, T., and T. Tomczak. 2009. "Erkenntnistheoretische basis der marketingwissenschaft." In *Qualitative Marktforschung*, eds. R. Buber and H. Holzmüller, 2nd ed, 65–79. Gabler, Wiesbaden.

Fraker, H. 2013. *The Hidden Potential of Sustainable Neighborhoods: Lessons from Low-Carbon Communities*. Washington, D.C: Island Press

Gaddis, P.O. 2000. "Business Schools: Fighting the Enemy Within." *Strategy and Business* 21, no. 4, pp. 51–57.

Generation Investment Management. 2012. *Sustainable Capitalism*. Retrieved June 13, 2019, from https://genfound.org/media/1136/advocacy-3-sustainable-capitalism.pdf

Generation Investment Management. 2019. *Sustainability Trends 2019*. Retrieved from https://generationim.com/sustainability-trends/sustainability-trends-2019/

Gentile, M.C. 2010. *Giving Voice to Values*. New Haven, CT: Yale University Press.

Ghoshal, S. 2005. "Bad Management Theories are Destroying Good Management Practices." *Academy of Management Learning and Education* 4, no. 1, pp. 75–91.

Giacalone, R.A., and K.R. Thompson. 2006. "Business Ethics and Social Responsibility Education: Shifting the Worldview." *Academy of Management Learning and Education* 5, no. 3, pp. 266–277.

Gloeckler, G. 2013. "MBA Rankings: Top Schools for Sustainability." Available at: https://businessweek.com/articles/2013-01-22/mba-rankings-top-schools-for-sustainability#r=blg-s (accessed 16 April 2013).

Gleiser, M. 2016. "ExxonMobil Vs. The World." NPR, https://npr.org/sections/13.7/2016/11/30/503825417/exxonmobil-vs-the-world

Gore, A., and D. Blood. 2011. "A Manifesto for Sustainable Capitalism." Retrieved June 13, 2019, from https://algore.com/news/a-manifesto-for-sustainable-capitalism

Graham, J.R., C.R. Harvey, and S. Rajgopal. 2005. "The Economic Implications of Corporate Financial Reporting." *Journal of Accounting and Economics*, 40, no. 1, 3–73. https://doi.org/10.1016/j.jacceco.2005.01.002

Guille'n, M. 2001. *The Limits of Convergence: Globalization and Organizational Change in Argentina, South Korea, and Spain*. Princeton, NJ: Princeton University Press.

Hambrick, D.C. 1994. "What If the Academy Really Mattered?", 1993 Presidential Address. *Academy of Management Review* 19, no. 1, pp. 11–16.

Haque, U. 2011. *The New Capitalist Manifesto: Building a Disruptively Better Business*. Harvard Business Review Press.

Henisz, W. 2011. "Leveraging the Financial Crisis to Fulfill The Promise of Progressive Management." *Academy of Management Learning & Education* 10, no. 2, pp. 289–321.

Daly, H. 2016. *From Uneconomic Growth to a Steady-state Economy*. Cheltenham, UK: Edward Elgar Publication

Holland, K. 2009. *"Is It Time to Retrain B-Schools?."* 15 March, pp. BU1.

Hommel, U., and H. Thomas. 2014. "Research on Business Schools: Themes, Conjectures, and Future Directions." In *The Institutional Development of Business Schools*, eds. A.M. Pettigrew, E. Cornuel, and U. Hommel, 6–35. Oxford, UK: Oxford University Press.

Hommel, U., M. Painter-Morland, and J. Wang. 2012. "Gradualism Prevails and Perception Outbids Substance." *Global Focus* 6, no. 20, pp. 30–33.

Huang, T. 2019, June. *Tracking China's Debt-to-Equity Swap Program: "Great Cry and Little Wool" | PIIE*. Retrieved July 3, 2019, from https://piie.com/blogs/china-economic-watch/tracking-chinas-debt-equity-swap-program-great-cry-and-little-wool

Hudson, R. 2005. "Towards Sustainable Economic Practices, Flows and Spaces: Or is the Necessary Impossible and the Impossible Necessary?" *Sustainable Development* 13, no. 4, pp. 239–252.

Ikerd, J. 2005. *Sustainable Capitalism: A Matter of Common Sense*. Bloomfield, CT: Kumarian Press Inc.

Integrated Reporting. September 2011. *Towards Integrated Reporting-Communicating Value in the 21st Century*. Retrieved July 7, 2019, from http://integratedreporting.org/resource/discussion-paper/

Jeffrey P., and T.F. Christina. 2002. "The End of Business Schools? Less Success than Meets the Eye." *Academy of Management Learning & Education* 1, no. 1, pp. 78–95.

Johnson, H.G. 1971. "The Keynesian Revolution and the Monetarist Counter-Revolution." *The American Economic Review* 61, no. 2, pp. 1–14.

Jun, M. 2019. "Greening the Belt and Road is Essential to our Climate's Future | World Economic Forum." Retrieved July 2, 2019, from https://weforum.org/agenda/2019/07/belt-and-road-climate-future-change-green/

Khurana, R. 2007. *From Higher Aims to Hired Hands.* Princeton, NJ: Princeton University Press.

King, M.E. 2016. "From Financial Capitalism to Sustainable Capitalism." *The CPA Journal; New York* 86, no. 6, pp. 4–6.

Kiron, D., N. Kruschwitz, K. Haanæs and I.V.S. Velken. 2012. "Sustainability Nears a Tipping Point." *MIT Sloan Management Review* 53, pp. 69–74.

Lämsä, A.M., M. Vehkaperä, T. Puttonen, and H.L. Pesonen. 2008. "Effect of Business Education on Women and Men Students' Attitudes on Corporate Responsibility in Society." *Journal of Business Ethics* 82, pp. 45–58.

Lawrence Livermore National Laboratory. 2018. "Visualizing U.S. Energy Use in One Massive Chart." Retrieved July 3, 2019, from https://visualcapitalist.com/visualizing-u-s-energy-use-in-one-giant-chart/

Leroy, P., H. van den Bosch, and S. Ligthart. 2001. "The Role of Project-Based Learning in the "Political and Social Sciences of the Environment" Curriculum at Nijmegen University." *International Journal of Sustainability in Higher Education* 2, no. 1, pp. 8–20.

Lewis, M. 1982. *Liars' Poker.* W.W. Norton & Company.

Lewis, M. 2010. *The Big Short, Inside the Doomsday Machine.* W. W. Norton & Company.

Li, X., X. Liu, and Y. Wang. 2015. *A Model of China's State Capitalism.* IDEAS Working Paper Series from RePEc; St. Louis. Retrieved from http://search.proquest.com/docview/1698498228?rfr_id=info%3Axri%2Fsid%3Aprimo

Lin, B. 2018, May. "China is a Renewable Energy Champion. But It's Time for a New Approach | World Economic Forum." Retrieved July 3, 2019, from https://weforum.org/agenda/2018/05/china-is-a-renewable-energy-champion-but-its-time-for-a-new-approach/

Lin, L.W. 2017. "A Network Anatomy of Chinese State-Owned Enterprises." *World Trade Review* 16, no. 4, pp. 583–600. https://doi.org/10.1017/S1474745617000210

Lin, L.W., and C.J. Milhaupt. 2011. "We are the (National) Champions: Understanding the Mechanisms of State Capitalism in China." *SSRN Electronic Journal.* https://doi.org/10.2139/ssrn.1952623

Lin, S., H. Xia, and I. Bardhan. 2019. "The Effect of Audit Committee Financial Expertise on Earnings and Expectations Management Tactics to Meet or Beat Analyst Expectations in the post-SOX era." Working Paper.

Lindvall, J. 2006. "The Politics of Purpose: Swedish Economic Policy after the Golden Age." *Comparative Politics* 38, no. 3, pp. 253–272.

Lubman, S. 2012. "China Real Time: China's State Capitalism: The Real World Implications." *Dow Jones Institutional News.* New York, NY.

Retrieved from http://search.proquest.com/docview/2127325982/citation/ AFA93BEAEC454D30PQ/1

Martin, R.L., and S. Osberg. 2007. "Social Entrepreneurship: The Case for Definition." *Stanford Social Innovation Review* 5, no. 2, pp. 28–39.

McKinsey. 2011. "Long-Term Capitalism." Available at: http://mckinsey.com/ Capitalism/Roger_Ferguson.aspx (accessed 12 May 2011).

McNally, C.A. 2013. "How Emerging Forms of Capitalism Are Changing the Global Economic Order." Retrieved from http://search.proquest.com/ docview/1373466218/A777BB441BFD454CPQ/5

Meadows, D.H., D.L. Meadows, J. Randers, and W.W. Behrens III. 1972. *The Limits to Growth*. New York, NY: Universe Books.

Mellar, T. 2010. "Válaszút előtt a makroökonómia? [Macroeconomics facing a choice?]." *Közgazdasági Szemle* VolumeLVII, pp. 591–611.

Mintzberg, H. 2004. *Managers Not MBAs: A Hard Look At the Soft Practice of Managing and Management Development*. San Francisco, CA: Berrett-Koehler.

Mitroff, I. 2004. "An Open Letter to the Deans and the Faculties of American Business Schools." *Journal of Business Ethics* 54, no. 2, pp. 185–l89.

Moczar, J. 2010/a. Paul A. Samuelson, a közgazdaságtan utolsó nagy generalistája (1915–2009) [Paul A. Samuelson, the last great generalist of economics], Matematika és közgazdaságtan. *Közgazdasági Szemle* Volume LVII, pp. 371–379.

Muff, K., T. Dyllick, M. Drewell, J. North, P. Shrivastava, and J. Haertle. 2013. *Management Education for the World: A Vision for Business Schools Serving People and Planet*. Northampton, MA: Edward Elgar Publishing.

Noguchi, F., J.R. Guevara, and R. Yorozu. 2015. "Communities in Action: Lifelong Learning for Sustainable Development." Hamburg: UIL. Available at: http://bit.ly/1NxGncP

Office for Labour Statistics, US Department of Labour. 2009. "Employment and Wages Online Annual Averages."

Ollivaud, P., Y. Guillemette, and D. Turner. 2018. "Investment As A Transmission Mechanism from Weak Demand To Weak Supply and the Post-Crisis Productivity Slowdown." OECD Economics Department Working Papers, No. 1466, OECD Publishing, Paris. https://doi.org/10.1787/0c62cc26-en

Painter-Morland, M.J. 2015. "Philosophical Assumptions Undermining Responsible Management Education." *Journal of Management Development* 34, no. 1, pp. 61–75.

Pettigrew, A. 2001. "Management Research After Modernism." *British Journal of Management* 12, no. S1, pp. S61–S70.

Pezzey, J.C.V., and M.A. Toman. 2002. "Progress and Problems in the Economics of Sustainability." In *International Yearbook of Environmental and Resource Economics 2002/3*, eds. T. Tietenberg and H.F. Cheltenham. 165–232. UK: Edward Elgar.

Pfeffer, J., and C.T. Fong. 2002. "The End of Business Schools? Less Success than Meets the Eye." *Academy of Management Learning and Education* 1, pp. 78–95.

Pfeffer, J., and C.T. Fong. 2004. "The Business School 'Business': Some Lessons from the US experience." *Journal of Management Studies* 41, no. 8, pp. 1501–1520.

Pfeffer, J., and C.T. Fong. 2004. "The Business School "Business": Some Lessons from the U.S. experience." Stanford Graduate School of Business Research Paper Series, 2004.

Piketty, T., and A. Goldhammer. 2014. *Capital in the Twenty-First Century.* Cambridge, Massachusetts: The Belknap Press of Harvard University Press.

Porter, M.E., M.R. and Kramer. 2011. "Creating Shared Value." *Harvard Business Review* 89, nos. 1/2, pp. 62–66.

Rajan, R.G. 2005. "Has Financial Development Made the World Riskier." Paper presented at The Greenspan Era: Lessons for the Future, Federal Reserve Bank of Kansas Symposium, Jackson Hole, WY. http://imf.org

Rasche, A., D.U. Gilbert, and I. Schedel. 2013. "Cross-Disciplinary Ethics Education in MBA Programs, Rhetoric or Reality?" *Academy of Management Learning and Education* 12, no. 1, pp. 71–85.

Reid, A., P. Petocz, and P. Taylor. 2009. "Business Students' Conception of Sustainability." *Sustainability* 1, no. 3, pp. 662–673.

Reid, A., and P. Petocz. 2006. "University Lecturers' Understanding of Sustainability." *Higher Education* 51, no. 1, pp. 105–123.

Reinhart, C.M., and K.S. Rogoff. 2008. "This Time is Different: A Panoramic View of Eight Centuries of Financial Crises, National Bureau of Economic Research." Working Paper 13882, Cambridge, MA. http://nber.org/papers/w13882

Robertson, J. 1999. "The New Economics of Sustainable Development." *Briefing for Policy Makers*. European Commission Report.

Roome, N. 2005. "Teaching Sustainability in a Global MBA: Insights from the One MBA." *Business Strategy and the Environment* 14, pp. 160–171.

Rusinko, C.A. 2010. "Integrating Sustainability in Management and Business Education." The *Academy of Management Learning and Education* 9, no. 3, pp. 507–519.

Russell, J. 2012. "When Philosophers Rule: The Platonic Academy and Statesmanship." *History of Political Thought* 33, no. 2, pp. 209–230.

Rynes, S.L., and D.L. Shapiro. 2005. "Public Policy and the Public Interest: What If We Mattered More?" Editors Forum. *Academy of Management Journal* 48, no. 6, pp. 925–927.

Scherer, A.G., G. Palazzo, and D. Seidl. 2013. "Managing Legitimacy in Complex and Heterogeneous Environments: Sustainable Development in a Globalized World." *Journal of Management Studies* 50, no. 2, pp. 259–284.

Schoemaker, P.J. 2008. "The Future Challenges of Business: Rethinking Management Education and Research." *California Management Review* 50, no. 3, pp. 119–139.

Schumacher, E. F. 1973. *Small is Beautiful: Economics As If People Mattered.* New York, NY: Harper & Row.

Scott, M. 2019, January. "The Global 100 difference | Corporate Knights." Retrieved July 3, 2019, from https://corporateknights.com/reports/2019-global-100/global-100-difference-15481154/

Seelos, C., and J. Mair. 2005. "Social Entrepreneurship: Creating New Business Models to Serve the Poor." *Business Horizons* 48, no. 3, pp. 241–246.

Simons, R. 2013. "The Business of Business School: Restoring a Focus on Competing to Win." *Capitalism and Society* 8, no. 1, pp. 1–37.

Slater, D.J., and H.R. Dixon-Fowler. 2010. "The Future of the Planet in the Hands of MBAs: An Examination of CEO MBA Education and Corporate Environmental Performance." *Academy of Management Learning and Education* 9, no. 3, pp. 429–441.

Starik, M., G. Rands, A.A. Marcus, and T.S. Clark. 2010. "Editorial: In Search of Sustainability in Management Education." *Academy of Management Learning & Education* 9, no. 3, pp. 377–383.

Starkey, K., A. Hatchuel, and S. Tempest. 2004. "Rethinking the Business School." *Journal of Management Studies* 41, no. 8, pp. 1521–1531.

Starkey, K., and S. Tempest. 2009. "The Winter of our Discontent: The Design Challenge for Business Schools." *The Academy of Management Learning & Education* 8, pp. 576–586.

Stathis, K.L. 2015. "Ocean Tomo Releases 2015 Annual Study of Intangible Asset Market Value." Retrieved July 3, 2019, from https://oceantomo.com/blog/2015/03-05-ocean-tomo-2015-intangible-asset-market-value/

Sterling, S. 2004. "Higher Education, Sustainability and the Role of Systemic Learning." In *Higher Education and the Challenge of Sustainability: Contestation, Critique, Practice, and Promise,* eds. P. Corcoran and A. Wals. Dordrecht: Kluwer Academic.

Stibbe, A. 2009. *The Handbook of Sustainability Literacy: Skills for A Changing World.* Totnes: Green Books.

Stiglitz, J.E. 2012. *The Price of Inequality: How Today's Divided Society Endangers Our Future.* New York, NY: W.W. Norton & Co.

Swaen, V., P. de Woot, and D. de Callataÿ. 2011. "The Business School of The Twenty-First Century: Educating Citizens to Address the New World Challenges." In *Business Schools and their Contribution to Society,* eds. M. Morsing, and A. Sauquet Rovira, 175–192. London: Sage.

Schweickart, D. January 1, 2009. "Is Sustainable Capitalism an Oxymoron?" *Perspectives on Global Development and Technology* 8, nos. (2–3), 559–580. doi:10.1163/156914909X424033

Steffen, W., J. Rockström, K. Richardson, T.M. Lenton, C. Folke, D. Liverman, C.P. Summerhayes, A.D. Barnosky, S.E. Cornell, M. Crucifix, J.F. Donges, I. Fetzer, S.J. Lade, M. Scheffer, R. Winkelmann, and H.J. Schellnhuber. 2018. "Trajectories of the Earth System in the Anthropocene." Proceedings of the National Academy of Sciences 115, no. 33, 8252-8259. doi: 10.1073/pnas.1810141115

Tavares, R. 2018. *Companies Need To Be Born Socially Responsible. Here are 10 reasons why | World Economic Forum.* Retrieved July 2, 2019, from https://weforum.org/agenda/2018/03/companies-need-to-be-born-socially-responsible-here-s-why/

Teece, D. (2010). "Achieving Integration of the Business School Curriculum using the Dynamic Capabilities Framework." Draft v8, 3 May, Paper presented at the School of Business, Economics and Law at Gothenburg University, 12 April, 2011.

The Generation Foundation. 2015. *Allocating Capital for Long-Term Returns.*

The World Commission on Environment and Development. 1987. *Our Common Future*, ed. Gro Brundtland. Oxford, England: Oxford University Press.

Thomas, H., and A.D. Wilson. 2011. "Physics Envy, Cognitive Legitimacy or Practical Relevance: Dilemmas in the Evolution of Management Research in the UK." *British Journal of Management* 22, no. 3, pp. 443–456.

Thomas, H., and E. Cornuel. 2011. "Business School Futures: Evaluation and Perspectives." *Journal of Management Development* 30, no. 5, pp. 444–450.

Truscheit, A., and C. Otte. 2007. "Sustainable Games People Play: Teaching Sustainability Skills with the Aid of the Role-Play, NordWestPower." In *Teaching Business Sustainability. Volume 2: Cases, Simulations and Experiential Approaches*, ed. C. Galea, 164–170. Sheffield: Greenleaf.

United Nations. 1992. *Earth Summit – Agenda 21*

United Nations. Global Sustainable Report for 2014.

United Nations. Global Sustainable Report for 2015.

United Nations. Global Sustainable Reports for 2016.

United Nations. The Future We Want –Resolution adopted by the General Assembly on 27 July 2012.

United Nations. 2015. *Transforming our World: The 2030 Agenda for Sustainable Development.*

Ward, B., R.J. Dubos, and United Nations Conference on the Human Environment. 1972. *Only One Environment: The Care and Maintenance of A Small Planet.* New York, NY: W.W. Norton.

Watts, E. 2007. "Creating the Academy: Historical Discourse and the Shape of Community in the Old Academy." *The Journal of Hellenic Studies* 127, 106–122.

WBCSD. 2012. "Peter Bakker keynotes at Prince's Accounting for Sustainability Project Annual Event." Available at: http://wbcsd.org/Pages/eNews/eNewsDetails.aspx?ID=15305&NoSearchContextKey=true

WCED. 1987. *World Commission on Environment and Development, 'Our Common Future'*. Oxford: Oxford University Press.

Werhane, P.W., and M. Painter-Morland, eds. 2011. *Leadership, Gender and Organization*. Dordrecht: Springer.

Wilson, D.C., and H. Thomas. 2012. "The Legitimacy of the Business of Business Schools: What's the Future?" *Journal of Management Development* 31, no. 4, pp. 368–376. ISSN 0262-1711

World Bank Group. 2017. *China's Systematic Country Diagnostic: Towards A More Inclusive and Sustainable Development*.

World Commission for Environment and Development WCED. 1987. *'Our Common Future'*. Oxford: Oxford University Press.

Wright, R.E. 2010. "Teaching History in Business Schools: An Insider's View." *Academy of Management Learning & Education* 9, 697–700.

Zhuo, T. 2016. "Sustainable Capitalism Is the Next Big Thing in Investing." Retrieved June 13, 2019, from Entrepreneur website: https://entrepreneur.com/article/269813

About the Authors

Marcus Goncalves, Ed.D., Ph.D.

Marcus Goncalves is an international business researcher focusing most of his research on international entrepreneurship and MNEs internationalization modes of entry, particularly Lusophone-African and frontier markets' internationalization strategies. He is also an international management consultant with more than 30 years of experience in the United States, Latin America, Europe, the Middle East, and Asia. He holds a doctorate in Educational Leadership from Boston University and a Ph.D. in Business from the University of Saint Joseph, Macao, China S.A.R. He has more than 45 books published in the United States, many translated into Portuguese, German, Chinese, Korean, Japanese, and Spanish. He is often invited to speak on international business, global trade, international management, and organizational development subjects worldwide. He is an Associate Professor of the Practice at Boston University/MET in Boston, MA. Dr. Goncalves can be contacted via email at marcusg@bu.edu or marcusg@mgcgusa.com.

Harry Xia, DBA

Harry Xia is an Associate Professor and Director of Graduate Business Programs at the Craig School of Business of the California State University, Fresno (Fresno State). He had held key management positions in finance and marketing for multinational corporations in the United States and the Asia Pacific for almost 20 years before joining Fresno State and still serves as an active business consultant and advisor to companies in the greater China region and its surrounding areas. His primary research interests include corporate finance, international business, and corporate governance. His research has been published in numerous journals and conference proceedings. He holds a Doctor of Business Administration from the Hong Kong Polytechnic University and a Master of Hospitality Management from the University of Houston in Texas. Dr. Xia can be contacted via email at hxia@mail.fresnostate.edu.

Mario Svigir, Ph.D.

Mario Svigir is a researcher and lecturer of international and sustainable economics at a variety of business schools in Eastern Europe. He holds a doctorate in Economics. Dr. Svigir collaborates extensively, as contracted expert, with the European Commission (E.C.), U.S. Agency for International Development (USAID), the International Training Centre of the International Labor Organization (ITC-ILO) in Turin, Italy, and the World Bank International Bank for Reconstruction and Development (IBRD) on projects dealing with growth, governance, economic policy, equality, cohesion, and sustainability. As a macroeconomic advisor, he steers actions related to the establishment of a global coalition of sovereign wealth funds and potential establishment of U.S.- and China-based sovereign wealth funds. His ideas for a more effective global economy for the 21st century are related to better deployment of the relationship between real and financial economics and proper adoption of the digital postmodern outlook of an economy, from local to a global level, toward its socially and environmentally more sustainable setup. After spending years of investigating the structural transformation of the European Union, he is an avid promoter of the need for its centralized innovation transformation policy. He can be contacted, in Croatia, via email at mariosvigir@yahoo.com.

Index

OTHER TITLES IN OUR ECONOMICS AND PUBLIC POLICY COLLECTION

Philip Romero, The University of Oregon and Jeffrey Edwards, North Carolina A&T State University, Editors

- *Universal Basic Income and the Threat to Democracy as We Know It* by Peter Nelson
- *Negotiation Madness* by Peter Nelson
- *Macroeconomics, Second Edition* by David G. Tuerck
- *Economic Renaissance In the Age of Artificial Intelligence* by Apek Mulay
- *Foreign Direct Investment* by Leena Ajit Kaushal

Announcing the Business Expert Press Digital Library

Concise e-books business students need for classroom and research

This book can also be purchased in an e-book collection by your library as

- a one-time purchase,
- that is owned forever,
- allows for simultaneous readers,
- has no restrictions on printing, and
- can be downloaded as PDFs from within the library community.

Our digital library collections are a great solution to beat the rising cost of textbooks. E-books can be loaded into their course management systems or onto students' e-book readers.
The **Business Expert Press** digital libraries are very affordable, with no obligation to buy in future years. For more information, please visit **www.businessexpertpress.com/librarians**. To set up a trial in the United States, please email **sales@businessexpertpress.com**.